"Chris Warner is living proof that courage and intellect provide a powerful leadership combination. He and Don Schmincke serve as outstanding guides for exploring what it takes to lead an organization into difficult and uncharted terrain. If you're an executive who searches for the occasional inspirational gut-check, this book is a must for your shelf."

—David Callahan, executive editor,
SmartCEO Magazine

"At last, something new has been written about leadership. The authors skillfully bridge the gulf between what is required of leaders in life-and-death situations scaling the world's highest peaks and the more mundane, but sometimes no less scary, halls of corporate America."

—Cathy A. Trower, Ph.D., research director, co-principal investigator, Collaborative On Academic Careers in Higher Education (COACHE), Harvard University, Graduate School of Education

High Altitude Leadership

High Altitude Leadership

What the World's Most Forbidding Peaks Teach Us About Success

Chris Warner
Don Schmincke

WILEY

John Wiley & Sons, Inc.

Copyright © 2009 by Chris Warner and Don Schmincke. All rights reserved.

Published by Jossey-Bass
A Wiley Imprint
989 Market Street, San Francisco, CA 94103-1741—www.josseybass.com

No part of this publication may be reproduced, stored in a retrieval system, or transmitted in any form or by any means, electronic, mechanical, photocopying, recording, scanning, or otherwise, except as permitted under Section 107 or 108 of the 1976 United States Copyright Act, without either the prior written permission of the publisher, or authorization through payment of the appropriate per-copy fee to the Copyright Clearance Center, Inc., 222 Rosewood Drive, Danvers, MA 01923, 978-750-8400, fax 978-646-8600, or on the Web at www.copyright.com. Requests to the publisher for permission should be addressed to the Permissions Department, John Wiley & Sons, Inc., 111 River Street, Hoboken, NJ 07030, 201-748-6011, fax 201-748-6008, or online at www.wiley.com/go/permissions.

Readers should be aware that Internet Web sites offered as citations and/or sources for further information may have changed or disappeared between the time this was written and when it is read.

Limit of Liability/Disclaimer of Warranty: While the publisher and author have used their best efforts in preparing this book, they make no representations or warranties with respect to the accuracy or completeness of the contents of this book and specifically disclaim any implied warranties of merchantability or fitness for a particular purpose. No warranty may be created or extended by sales representatives or written sales materials. The advice and strategies contained herein may not be suitable for your situation. You should consult with a professional where appropriate. Neither the publisher nor author shall be liable for any loss of profit or any other commercial damages, including but not limited to special, incidental, consequential, or other damages.

Jossey-Bass books and products are available through most bookstores. To contact Jossey-Bass directly call our Customer Care Department within the U.S. at 800-956-7739, outside the U.S. at 317-572-3986, or fax 317-572-4002.

Jossey-Bass also publishes its books in a variety of electronic formats. Some content that appears in print may not be available in electronic books.

Library of Congress Cataloging-in-Publication Data

Warner, Chris, 1964-
   High altitude leadership : what the world's most forbidding peaks teach us about success /
Chris Warner, Don Schmincke. — 1st ed.
      p.   cm.
   Includes bibliographical references.
   ISBN 978-0-470-34503-0 (cloth)
      1. Leadership. 2. Success in business.   I. Schmincke, Don, 1956-   II. Title.
   HD57.7.W3685   2009
   658.4'092—dc22

                                                                    2008034927

Printed in the United States of America
FIRST EDITION
HB Printing   10 9 8 7 6 5 4 3 2 1

Contents

To our wives for encouraging us
to explore the highest peaks
And to our young children
who we hope will climb even higher

Preface

We never expected to write a book together. In fact, business leadership didn't seem to be something we were fated for. Don is a scientist and an engineer, not a management guru. He graduated from MIT and Johns Hopkins University with research ranging from simulating timing systems for the navy's nuclear missile systems at Draper Laboratories, to studying atmospheric effects on satellite frequencies at the Applied Physics Laboratory, to automating the Harvard/MIT biomedical laboratory (his thesis research published in the *Journal of Medical Instrumentation*) and helping pioneer fourth-generation medical imaging technology. While at Hopkins, he became fascinated with how humans organize and perform in groups, and even more fascinated by the high failure rates of management consulting and leadership theories trying to help organizations perform better.

Using anthropology and evolutionary genetics, Don discovered that most management theories fail during implementation due to biological factors. He then developed remarkably effective, and controversial, methods for producing exceptional organizational performance. Unearthing the origins of management behavior flies in the face of many modern business theories, but it apparently struck a chord with CEOs worldwide. Today, over seventy-five hundred CEOs have found Don's biological leadership applications refreshingly irreverent and revolutionary for bottom-line impact in their organizations.

Don founded The SAGA Leadership Institute in 1990 to continue his research and offer corporate training programs where executives discover why popular management theories fail to work and what to do for success. They learn why throwing poetic visions, wordsmithed mission statements, or idealistic value statements at primal, ego-driven turf wars is senseless. Managers also find out why forcing employees to "forget the past" with group hugs and touchy-feely training programs doesn't reduce backbiting, hidden agendas, and other profit-sapping behaviors for very long. With the myths dispelled, managers are primed to learn what does work—and has for thousands of years.

That is how Don, the engineer and scientist, became an established management consultant renegade, author, and keynote speaker. His work has been published a hundred times in the past eighteen months, seen on CNN, and written about in the *Wall Street Journal, USA Today,* and other national media. Today Don is one of the top speakers for the world's largest CEO membership organization. Every year he flies 200,000 miles to conferences where he is either a keynote speaker, training over seven hundred CEOs in his workshops, or working with clients in every imaginable organization, from the Department of Defense to large and small corporations.

Ironically, Don's eventual study of management behavior was inadvertent, much like his meeting Chris Warner in the Andes. At that time, Don was searching once again to validate genetic and anthropological leadership methods. His first book, *The Code of the Executive,* based on ancient Samurai executive training techniques, was already published in ten languages, and he was ready for another project. He had teased ancient secrets out of old manuscripts and discovered insights from several hundred genetic publications, but he wanted yet another new and unique leadership laboratory to learn what really does work. He listened to hundreds of motivational speakers and read as many of the thirty-five thousand business books published annually as he could. But in the end, he found little that was unique or different.

That all changed on a mountaineering expedition in the Andes as part of the Climb for Hope's fundraiser for breast cancer research at Johns Hopkins. The expedition was sponsored by Earth Treks, Chris's company. Don had pursued expeditions for years in the Himalayas, Africa, Indonesia, and other remote regions to advance his leadership research, but on this one he met expedition leader Chris Warner. Don recalls it this way:

> I really didn't know much about Chris. I was just extremely concerned about it being five degrees below zero and trying to climb ice at almost twenty thousand feet on an active volcano. You could say I was preoccupied with just staying alive. But I noticed something about Chris and his team. They were tight, focused, and professional. They were also fresh off another expedition which was a leadership development seminar for the Wharton School of Business. I asked Chris how he led teams like this in such extreme environments. He shared with me his experience of high performance teams tackling the world's most forbidding mountains. He also told me about dysfunctional teams collapsing under the strain of the challenge. The consequences were always dramatic. After hearing him analyze these leadership experiences, I knew I found the laboratory for my next book. It would be on high altitude leadership: leadership insights beyond what had typically been published by studying those who lead teams in the riskiest and most extremely challenging situations encountered in death zone environments. I approached Chris about the idea of doing a book together, and he quickly jumped on it. We both were teaching the same things, but in different classrooms.

Chris's story is different. He learned to lead the hard way. At age eighteen, he was taking teenagers out of the maximum security prison in New Jersey and leading them on six-month rehabilitative wilderness adventures. After years of banging heads with delinquents, he rehabbed himself by becoming a mountaineering guide and entrepreneur.

In 1990 he started Earth Treks with all the money he could scrape together: a whopping $592. Today Earth Treks operates three of the nation's largest indoor climbing gyms, a rock and ice climbing school, and an international mountaineering guide service. Chris has led over 150 international mountaineering expeditions and is one of only nine American climbers who have summited the world's two tallest mountains: Mount Everest and K2.

Earth Treks' gross revenue has grown 300 percent in the past three years. It now has over 175 employees and serves tens of thousands of customers every year. It is one of the largest companies in a tough niche industry. With all of its peers being privately held corporations, it's impossible to tell where Earth Treks ranks, but with growth like this, and earnings before interest, depreciation, and amortization above 20 percent, it's an admirable business to own. All this growth keeps happening even though in 2000, Chris's employees commandeered his desk and unplugged his phone; they figured he wasn't using either.

Based on this entrepreneurial success and Chris's international climbing reputation, Earth Treks was chosen in 2000 to guide leadership development expeditions for the Wharton School of Business. Each year Earth Treks' guides lead nearly a hundred M.B.A. candidates on mountaineering expeditions to the Andes and Africa. Chris's unique approach to leadership has led to a number of television projects. He guided the first reality TV show filmed on Mount Everest, hosted a leadership and risk-taking-themed special for the History Channel, and most recently partnered with NBC to produce a film of his successful K2 expedition. Chris was the field producer and expedition leader and, like everyone else on the small team, was a cameraman and climber/actor on this Emmy-nominated project. When Chris is in the country, he shares his tales of high altitude leadership with Fortune 500 companies and business schools as a keynote speaker or part of longer workshops. For more than twenty-five years, Chris has been a student of leadership, a teacher of leadership, and a leader.

Climbing together, we knew there was synergy in our leadership experiences. As we explored ideas, we kept stumbling on the links between validated biological leadership insights and death zone mountaineering experiences. What began as a conversation in a remote mountain hut grew into experiments with groups in the field. We dragged leaders we admired into the conversation. With increasing clarity, we retested and proved the concepts at corporate retreats and when we spoke to business and leadership groups. As the ideas resonated, we felt compelled to share our hard-earned lessons with a bigger audience. The result is in this book you're holding.

Acknowledgments

From Don:

The work that I do is powerful only if powerful people help me. I'm forever indebted to the staff at The SAGA Leadership Institute. They have evolved to be the strongest team I could ask for. I'm particularly grateful for Eileen Gwin, who took over as managing director, and Umar Hameed, who relieved me of an infinite number of business development tasks so I could pursue much-needed research and publishing opportunities. I also acknowledge Donna Delovich for assuming the challenging role of financial manager at the institute, filling a gap I spent so long creating. Special thanks to Bonnie Greenberg and Ann Ulick for keeping me on the right plane to the right city in the right hotel, among a thousand other details. I'm also grateful to the Institute field staff who so willingly accommodated me on this quest over the years, especially Susan Barrett, Chris Bogden, Charlie Davis, Griff Hall, Darryl McCormick, and Jill Penaloza.

The foundations of this research were built with numerous individuals, clients, and other organizations with the patience to work with me and test outrageous theories. First, much appreciation is due to the many Institute clients who use us for their strategic planning, executive team development, and cultural alignment. Without them, we would not have the funding to continue our research. Second, special thanks to Cathy Trower, now at Harvard University, who inspired me to teach at Johns Hopkins and inflict my unconventional methods on innocent graduate students. And, finally, my work could not grow or be validated without testing it with the world's CEOs. I am very grateful to Vistage (TEC) and YPO, two of the largest CEO membership organizations worldwide, for allowing me to conduct hundreds of workshops and challenge their members over the years. This work is stronger coming out of that crucible. I'm particularly grateful for my own Vistage group in Baltimore. They never cut me a break. I hope they never will.

Thanks to Ken and Margie Blanchard who in our work together inspired me to continue writing, offered great advice on publishing more, and even edited some of my earlier work. They introduced me to Margret McBride, our agent for this book.

Ironically, thanks to my MIT fraternity, Alpha Delta Phi, a literary brotherhood. While there, I never thought I'd end up being an author. My MIT brothers have flown space shuttle missions and flipped too many technology companies to mention. As I write this, I'm further humbled by their infamous Las Vegas gambling endeavors portrayed in the movie *21*.

I attribute the freedom to explore new ideas to my mom, Audrey, who always supported my education even though she never really knew what I was doing (and still doesn't), and to my father, the late Don Sr., a high altitude leader who as a teenager survived the riskiest and most extremely challenging goal in a death zone situation: surviving the POW camps of the Korean War. I'll never know the stories that died with him or his fellow POWs. A rare band of heroes, they never bragged.

Finally, traveling a couple of hundred thousand miles each year is possible only with a strong base camp. Thanks to my wife, Mary, who followed me throughout Africa, the Himalayas, Indonesia, and wherever else I felt pulled to go. And to my kids, Rowan and Nolan, who I hope will travel farther than I ever did. (You see? By letting Dad travel several days a week, he was able to write another book!)

From Chris:
My leadership journey started at birth with trying to compete for a little attention in a family of six kids. My grandmother,

Kitty Patwell, gets a lot of credit for getting me excited about the woods. She let us fill her small house with hundreds of newts, turtles, and the occasional wild rabbit. As long as I took a handful of my two dozen cousins with me, we were allowed to wander for miles.

The first time I was lost in a blizzard was on a Christmas Day. I was five or six years old and was guiding a few cousins on a never-ending sledding adventure. An uncle finally found us hours after nightfall.

In middle school we started hiking the Appalachian Trail, just a few friends with no adults to slow us down. In high school I was sent back into the woods, along with eleven other kids and a parole officer. The idea was to scare us straight. I was hardly afraid. I was in awe. There were two outdoor educators leading our team, Joe Thomas and Rachel Holtzworth. The moment I met them, I knew how I was going to spend the rest of my life: taking people on adventures.

I climbed my first mountain when I was seventeen. It was the Grand Teton, some two thousand miles from home. I told my mother, Barbara Warner, that I was heading off to college a few weeks early. Instead I hitchhiked to Wyoming. When I finally told her what I did, she had no concept of what climbing the Grand Teton meant. "Barbara, I'll translate it for you," said my all-knowing Uncle Rodie. "'Grand Tetons' is French for big boobs."

At eighteen, I applied for a job with the same outdoor organization that worked with my high school. Project USE was led by Phil Costello, the most charismatic leader I've ever met. He was a former reconnaissance marine who had no conception of the impossible, the impractical, or the impact he was having on a generation of educators. I couldn't have asked for a better mentor.

When Outward Bound opened an urban-based program in Baltimore in 1986, Phil asked me to help him get it rolling. The first course started when the sheriff arrived with two kids in handcuffs in the back of his car. He gave the kids to me and sped away.

In 1987, Dan Jenkins and I drove, then hitchhiked, and finally flew to the mountains of Peru. In two months we summited seven of ten big peaks. In 1989 Dan, Austin Weiss, and I headed to the Indian Himalayas. Those experiences taught me how to handle myself in the face of great risks.

In the early 1990s, I realized that working with hard-core kids was wearing me down, so I started Earth Treks, a climbing guide service. Tricia and Keith Hamilton were the first employees. ET would not have survived the first ten years without Tricia's hard work and leadership.

Those formative experiences taught me what a leader should be. It was the next fifteen years that taught me how to be the leader I now wanted to be. Through this never-ending second stage, I've climbed with hundreds of partners, each teaching me in some important way. In the course of the growth of Earth Treks, I've worked with nearly a thousand employees. It would read like a telephone book if I listed just the best. A few should be acknowledged, though, because of their continuous insistence that we live our values: Dan Jenkins, Travis Batemen, Brian Hughes, Chris Jenkins, Scot Heidtman, Nelson Laur, Chris Everett, Suzy Quintavalle, Charlotte Jouett, and Matt Bosley, who have all been a big part of the team for more than seven years.

Equally important are my mentors, the group that takes my crazy calls and finds a way to squash the bad ideas and give life to the few good ones: Joe DeFrancis, Kevin Maloney, Brian Sheahan, and Tricia Hamilton.

And then there are the academics and deep thinkers who challenge my perceptions and force me to learn how to teach these leadership concepts to others: Syl Mathis and Austin Paulson are the best guides and educators I've ever met. Mike Useem, Jeff Klein, Preston Cline, and Evan Wittenberg (now at Google), and the many brave and wise mountaineers at the

University of Pennsylvania's Wharton School, have given me plenty of chances to perfect my schtick. Rod "K2" Richardson, Doug Bruns, and many more leaders have shared their wisdom and time with me. We miss Rod terribly. He survived countless battles, only to have his life taken from us in Baghdad.

I owe endless gratitude to my extended family who have spent many sleepless nights praying for my safety and many warm evenings reminding me I'm just a Jersey punk. The biggest thanks go to my wife, Melinda, and our daughter, Wendy. We've traveled the world together, growing stronger with each step.

Both of us together thank the strong literary and PR agencies that supported us in this endeavor: Margret McBride, Donna DeGutis, John Mann, Rebecca Browning, Jane Wesman, Lori Ames, Brent Williams, Linden Gross, and their teams. This group played critical roles in the adventures of producing, publishing, and marketing this book.

Introduction

Leadership often sucks.

It's a risky, lonely role possessing nearly unbearable lows and fleeting highs. One moment leadership feels like the most deeply satisfying, life-enriching journey ever embarked on. Then fate's twist makes it an exhausting and stressful journey or a one-way ticket to cardiac arrest. Despite the downsides, leadership continues to be well marketed: leaders change the world, make a lot of money, are loved (if they want to be) or feared (if that's what they prefer). We have a hunch that you hope for the upsides from your leadership, whether you're leading a team, company, or your career. That's the reason you're reading this book.

We've been inspired by leadership marketing too. To deal with the responsibilities and challenges that have come with our roles over the years, we read the popular books, listened to the prevailing experts, and observed the work of top consultants. But after trying to apply their lessons in the field and hearing the war stories from CEOs we worked with, it became obvious that too many popular leadership models don't hold up in real organizations facing real challenges. We finally realized we were seeking answers in the wrong places.

We needed real answers.

After researching leadership success and failures scientifically, and testing various approaches, theories, and formulas in the most extreme situations, what have we learned? Despite the seductive, mainstream talking points of leadership theorists, there exists a rare and special breed of leaders who walk a different path. They are constantly pushing past current leadership trends in order to achieve the riskiest and most extremely challenging goals. We call these people *high altitude leaders*.

High altitude leaders:
Those who lead themselves and their teams to produce
peak performance in the face of extreme challenges
by overcoming the dangers not foreseen or addressed
by current, pop leadership theory

To our surprise, we discovered that high altitude leaders do something remarkably different. They aren't seduced by the latest leadership platitudes, clichés, or feel-good theories. They succeed instead by recognizing and surviving specific dangers—dangers that always emerge when these leaders take themselves or their teams to the highest levels of performance. If they cannot overcome these dangers, they know they will fail. In the most extreme situations, on the battlefield or in the mountains, these failures of leadership result in death.

In achieving peak performance as a high altitude leader, you also risk death. It could be the death of a career, project, team, or company, or, in extreme situations, someone's physical death. Learning the best way to succeed comes from studying the death zone.

Why Study Death Zone Leadership?

The death zone, an altitude above 26,000 feet, makes survival for a long period of time impossible because of the lack of available oxygen. Why did we choose death zone environments as a backdrop for these lessons? Certainly some people find stories about rescues, storms, frozen corpses, and avalanches pretty entertaining, but more important for our purposes, the dynamics of mountaineering provide tailor-made metaphors for business challenges.

Climbers bear a resemblance to entrepreneurs, career professionals, CEOs, and managers. They live passionately as part of a team confronting impossible odds. Some are deeply humble; others are psychotic narcissists. They come with all levels of competence, from naive wannabes to elite athletes. And when put to the test, they react like all of us: sometimes like heroes, other times like self-destructive villains.

Expeditions to the world's highest mountains provide the perfect laboratories to examine the dangers every leader faces. At these extreme altitudes success or failure is easily measured, and simple mistakes kill people.

> **When you are in the death zone, you can't grab a book**
> **to look for new theories,**
> **you can't dial a consultant, and motivational speakers are**
> **finally short of breath.**
> **Up here, the best teams emulate behaviors seen only**
> **in the highest-performing organizations—**
> **and the worst teams wallow in their dysfunction.**

The death zone provides a place to study leadership without the distraction or influence of consultants, trainers, or motivational speakers. This raw environment taxes the basic, primal instinct of our species because with stakes so high, any leadership mistake is fatal. Admittedly most leaders will never be challenged at these levels. But what can we learn that leaders everywhere can use to achieve something else, something different, something much higher than what they currently feel possible?

What You Will Learn

Where people can die or businesses can fail, high altitude leadership is needed. In fact, dangers threaten every leader at some point in their journey, even among groups that do the most boring work. The bad news is these dangers get magnified and new dangers emerge whenever a leader climbs higher. No doubt you already know some of these dangers. They cause headaches for every group and ruin the happiness all leaders earn.

In this book, we share what we've learned about the dangers encountered when getting to higher altitudes: why these dangers appear, what to do to survive them, and how to prevent them. We also share what we've personally learned about leading groups that have to perform at the peak of their ability in the most extreme circumstances. Seasoned leaders will learn how to avoid the dangers their careers and teams face. And if your hair is gray (or gone), you'll also have some tools to teach the next generation.

Specifically, we'll teach you how to handle the eight dangers that leaders regularly face in order to achieve a high altitude leader's peak performance: fear of death, selfishness, tool seduction, arrogance, lone heroism, cowardice, comfort, and gravity.

In the face of today's business challenges and tomorrow's unpredictable risks, companies need leaders who excel in the most extreme environments. With so much at risk, guiding your team and your career to the summit requires that you use every bit of your talent and every ounce of your strength. You need to be a high altitude leader.

We want you to be that leader. This book will help you. So strap on your crampons, and grab your ice ax. We're going to take the corner office to the cornice, the desk chair to the death zone, and your glassed-in conference room to the glacier. When you're finished you're going to have a whole different view of "peak" performance.

For Those Who Aren't Mountaineers

A brief note from Chris before you begin:

The publisher asked me to explain how an expedition works. Given the metaphorical context of this book, that sounds like a sensible question. But I'm stumped. How can you put so many variables into a simple definition? An expedition can be a simple affair or a complex initiative. For example, in the spring of 2001, I guided clients on the North Ridge of Mount Everest. We had forty thousand pounds of gear, two thousand rolls of toilet paper, and a budget approaching a half-million dollars. Fifteen of us reached the summit. Four months later, I climbed Mount Shisha Pangma, the world's fourteenth tallest mountain, all by myself! A cook and I brought about four hundred pounds of gear to base camp (and fewer than a dozen rolls of toilet paper). In total, the trip cost me less than six thousand dollars.

Which trip was more satisfying and more successful? Well, that depends on what you seek on the hill. I reached the summit on both mountains. On Everest I spent five days and four nights in the death zone, guiding clients to the summit, then managing a major rescue that became international news. On Shisha Pangma, I became the first American to solo a 26,000-foot peak, climbing completely alone from bottom to top without stopping to rest for thirty-four grueling hours.

On Everest, I climbed so that others could make their dreams come true. On Shisha Pangma, I climbed for myself.

Let me tell you some of the things that an expedition is not. It's not a purely competitive event, with impartial judges. It's not even always judged by reaching the summit. Some of the boldest climbs in history ascend geological features on a mountain, with the first ascensionists considering the summit superfluous.

Even with the sport's goals a little murky and judges sitting in distant armchairs, high altitude mountaineers are fiercely driven. We have to be. We play in a sport full of fatal dramas. Our history is defined by life-and-death epics. Our most talked-about statistics are measured by death. The death-to-summit ratio (the percentage of people dying versus those that summit) for Mount Everest (29,035 feet) is 1.8 percent; on the world's second-tallest mountain, K2 (28,253 feet), it is 23 percent. Mountaineers learn to fight with all their talents and strengths so they can survive.

An expedition is a journey of physical, emotional, and intellectual brutality that kicks the crap out of you and in which the opportunity for things going wrong is built into the formula. Combine real risk with unbearable cold, unwashed partners, and bad food, and you have an expedition.

Seeking high altitude leadership also promises to kick the crap out of you. Thankfully in business, you can eat better—and your partners usually shower.

High Altitude Leadership

K2, at 28,253 feet the world's second-tallest and arguably most dangerous peak

2007 Shared Summits K2 Expedition, Chris Warner

Danger #1

FEAR OF DEATH

Remember not to have a fatal accident, because the
community will think climbing is a dangerous thing,
your friends will be bummed . . . and you'll be dead.
*—Kitty Calhoun, America's top female mountaineer
in the 1990s, closing remarks at an
American Alpine Club lecture*

Time: July 20, 2007, Summit Day
Location: K2, Pakistan

4:45 A.M.: Vapor from my breath immediately freezes on my
beard. At twenty-five degrees below zero and 26,500 feet above
sea level, I'm lucky to be breathing at all. The three members of
our team are not using bottled oxygen, and at this altitude, there
is barely one-third the oxygen at sea level. With so little oxygen
reaching our brains and fingertips, we struggle to stay warm,
think straight, and climb higher. The list of reasons to turn
back keeps growing. We can see the final summit climb hanging
above us: 2,000 feet of twisting snow gullies, a nearly vertical
traverse below a hanging glacier, and a knife-edged ridgeline.
As we prepare for hours of physical and emotional endurance,
we know that everything will be demanded of us—if we make it
to the top at all. This is not just any mountain. It's K2: the
world's second-highest and most feared peak. For our team, this
day will be the ultimate test.

The Korean team struggles through the deep snow, barely 100 feet above us. Sucking bottled oxygen and teamed with three experienced Sherpas, they should be farther ahead. But at this altitude, simple problems become monumental challenges. They've reached a notoriously treacherous spot known as the Bottleneck. More than a dozen climbers have died there over the years, and the Koreans are rigging the first set of ropes, ensuring all our safety.

As I adjust my gear, I look up. Suddenly the Korean team's professional leader, Nima Nurbu Sherpa, a highly experienced climber who had summited Mount Everest six times, slips and falls. He rockets to the bottom of the Bottleneck, but slows as he toboggans across the only flat patch on the nearly vertical South Face. I hold my breath, expecting him to plant his ice ax and stop himself on this relatively modest slope.

But he doesn't.

To our horror, Nima slides off the edge and tumbles into the darkness. At our altitude, he will fall for several minutes before hitting the glacier 10,000 feet below us.

Nima is dead.

His body will never be recovered.

Leadership is a sweet delusion: so fragile, so easily sabotaged.

Whether on a mountain or at work, leading others can quickly become difficult and dangerous. You want so badly to influence positive change in your organization. You accept the title of leadership and purposefully trek upward, propelled by hope. In this exciting journey, you seek to be a great leader leading a great company to great altitudes. With best-selling books, inspirational trainings, and smartly dressed consultants, you expect to finally reach the summit and become—well, great.

Then you slip off the cliff into reality. Instead of things going your way, leadership becomes a burden as the world fails to cooperate with your dreams. In an instant, the threat of failure awakens you from the delusion. Luckily most of us don't tumble to our deaths if we stumble. But how you respond in the face of real dangers defines you as a leader.

Leadership destroys climbers on windswept slopes at 26,000 feet, and executives in comfortable conference rooms. It occurs during the death of great ideas and plans. When the hoped-for promotions or projects die, when commitments or sales aspirations breathe their last breath, the danger emerges: great fear.

Only now will your true greatness arise. Or not.

Will you freeze in the face of your fears? Or will you fight?

Great Fear: The Nemesis of Great Leadership

In a moment of great fear, action stops. We see it all the time. One client, a second-generation office product company, reached such a critical point. The CEO knew that future sales growth and expansion required a new channel or path to focus the company's attention and resources. After a series on on-site assessments and an off-site program, it was clear that the necessary plans for repositioning the company were being thwarted by two old-guard salesmen. These salesmen were great day-to-day performers, but they had no capacity for the strategic thinking needed to support the plan.

Obviously these salesmen were out of place on the executive team, and many on the executive team agreed. But when they faced the prospect of reassigning these salesmen, or even firing them, the CEO froze. And the high costs of inaction befell him. The company's founder (the CEO's dad) had hired these old-timers, and the CEO was too afraid to confront them. Although the executive team found the new strategy a much-needed breakthrough for getting to a new level of performance, this summit push failed because of the CEO's fear to take action. In a sense, he sabotaged his own company. Unable to accept his own weak leadership, he blamed the process instead. The CEO and his team were frozen in place, the summit not yet attainable.

Whether in an office or on a mountain, choosing to stay stuck in the safe world ensures losses of great opportunities to the ultimate strategy killer: fear. It stops staff from making great decisions, stops change agents from disrupting the status quo, and stops leaders from leading.

> *The desire for safety stands against every great and noble enterprise.*
>
> Tacitus, Roman philosopher

Is this so surprising? After all, traditional business education occurs safely in a safe classroom with safe books and a safely tenured professor. So when great decisions have to be made, who has the courage to step forward? In the face of impending danger and high risk, many leaders are deterred from their mission or stopped altogether, no matter how well they're educated or think they're ready for the challenge.

You will wrestle with the fear of death no matter what altitude you're at. But if you want to reach the summit, you must fight onward.

How Do You Tame Your Fear?

Let's consider Nima's death that fateful day on K2, a mountain that is known to be deadly. It certainly wasn't surprising that someone would die on that summit push, although I wouldn't have guessed it would be Nima, who was level-headed and highly experienced.

Nima's was the first mountaineering death many in our group of elite mountaineers had ever watched, and it was a particularly gruesome way to die. When Nima fell, with him went the group's strategy for fixing the three thousand feet of rope we needed to secure the summit climb. His team was supposed to fix the first thousand feet, our team would fix the middle thousand, and the Russians would fix the last thousand feet. Fixing these ropes creates risk and exhaustion, and sharing that risk and labor was the only logical and practical approach. Now our strategy was in disarray. Who even knew who had what section of ropes and the anchors we needed? Was Nima's pack loaded with critical pieces of the group's gear? The group froze.

When faced with fear, most people freeze up. Among humans, fear becomes the dominant biological response, and an estimated 90 percent of us freeze up when stressed.[2] In the moment, this causes all sorts of problems (we get hit by the oncoming train instead of stepping off the tracks), and in the long term, it can destroy us (it suppresses our sex drive, leads us to withdraw from friends and family, drives substance abuse and other self-destructive behaviors, and causes weight gain). When we freeze, our relationships and health suffer direct consequences.

Anything I've ever done that ultimately was worthwhile . . . initially scared me to death.[1]

Betty Bender,
American professor

We see the same effects of freezing up in teams. As fear races through a team, whether the fear of confronting coworkers or the fear of a failed project, team members withdraw, morale sinks, and whispered conversations and accusatory e-mails cause distrust. The rats start jumping off the ship, and the team self-destructs.

As leaders, we have to combat the freeze response and prevent it from taking root in our professional lives and the teams we lead. But how do you do this? When many high altitude leaders identify the moment they overcame the great fear that could have frozen them, they tell you they focused not on whether they succeeded or failed, but on the very fact that they acted in the face of great fear.

When the summit seems lost, when the risk of death is greatest, seize the opportunity to become a high altitude leader! At this moment 90 percent of your peers will fail, but the few possessing the fighter's instinct will leap the crevasse and continue the journey to the summit.

High altitude leaders tame fear in themselves, their teams, and their organizational cultures by taking decisive action.

Bruce Normand, climbing K2

2007 Shared Summits K2 Expedition, Chris Warner

How can you teach taking action? How do high altitude leaders consistently act in the face of real fear?

The way to get started is to quit talking and begin doing.

Walt Disney

SURVIVAL TIP: Embrace Death

*For the samurai to learn
There's only one thing,
One last thing—
To face death unflinchingly.*

Tsukahara Bokuden, noted swordsman

K2, Summit Day, continued

Stunned by Nima's death, we stop—not just our team of three but everyone else pushing to the summit: two dozen climbers from ten countries. All of us have come together at this point on this mountain because we need each other's help to succeed. And we are here on this particular day because it is one of very few this decade that has been forecast to be good enough to summit this peak.

Now, struck by the fear of death, our confidence slid off the edge with Nima. Each of us is facing a painful dilemma: if we don't continue climbing, we will miss the window in the weather—a certain failed climb for this coalition.

Listen! I tell myself. *If you didn't think this would happen, you're delusional. Are you going to let this stop you?*

In a moment of bitter realization, I choose to accept Nima's death and all the risks that lay ahead. K2 had already claimed the lives of sixty-four climbers. Nima was the sixty-fifth. On K2, the odds of survival are low; the odds of summiting are lower. Even if we do summit, the odds of survival get worse: one in seven of all who summit K2 die descending. If I want to summit, now is not the time to grieve, but to act. Someone has to take over the job of leading. It might as well be me. I pay my silent respects to Nima and climb on. When I reach his Nepali and Korean teammates, I pay my respects to them. Some of them are already descending, and some are immobilized, literally trapped by their fear on the steep slope. I untangle the ropes that were dropped when Nima fell. Then I tie on a new 200-foot section and begin climbing toward the summit. Below me, the other climbers are weighing their options.

We each had to accept the possibility of our death if we were to continue. If we didn't accept what we always knew was a possibility, we would fail. Soon most of us are heading upward.

Acting at that moment allowed eighteen climbers to stand on top of the world some thirteen hours later. After a brutally hard struggle, physically and emotionally, it became the most successful summit day in the history of K2, the most dangerous mountain in the world.

Chris knew, without needing to think it through, how to act. The freedom to act instead of freeze by accepting death was not new to Chris. Here's how he tells it:

In 2002 when I was first attempting K2, two climbers were killed. One was wiped out in a massive avalanche. The second slipped off an exposed ledge and bounced for five thousand vertical feet. I watched him fall. Every time his body slammed into the mountain, a splash of blood marked the spot. He was dead long before his body rolled to a stop, still five hundred feet above us. Five of us watched this horror unfold, but only two of us climbed to the body. It took us nearly twenty minutes to reach him. We knew he was dead, but still we had to place our fingers on his neck to check for a pulse. His eyes were open, but with his skull smashed, the eyes and nose and mouth were all slightly misplaced on his now graying face. Certain he had no pulse, we radioed his friends in base camp, telling them he was dead.

We all lost a friend, and it didn't seem appropriate that his teammates had to see him like this. He was so bloodied and twisted that it took a garbage bag and the covering of several tents to contain the blood and cover his body. Lifting his body to wrap him up, we were covered in his blood, and I steeled my stomach to keep from vomiting. That night I couldn't sleep. Every time I closed my eyes, his fall and our handling of his body replayed in an endless loop.

This was not my first experience with death. The first time someone died in my hands, I felt the person's soul leave his body and pass through my hands. It was surreal, to say the least. In that moment, I learned how to handle death as it occurs. We have one job, whether the person is a total stranger or an old friend. We need to push as much love into the person as we can. A departing soul deserves to be honored by the greatest human emotion, love, and it is our job to supply plenty of it.

Add those two deaths to the dozen or so I saw while guiding Everest and the random handful from other mountains, and I quickly learned how to deal with these tragedies. If I didn't fail to save that man's life (he died in my hands even though I was trying to save his life), I wouldn't have learned how to act when people I knew were dying. First, honor the dead. Then honor the survivors in a way that inspires others to be their best.

That morning on K2, we all stopped as Nima slid to his death. We were struck with fear. I imagine that most of us were too consumed with our own questions of survival to think too much about Nima or his teammates. Nima's teammates, already shattered by his death, still had to survive a dangerous descent and break the news to Nima's family. When I saw him tumble off the edge, I felt the fear but still knew what I had to do. First, I honored his soul. While we were waiting for his team to sort themselves out and start to descend, I questioned my desire and our strategy for climbing this deadly mountain. It took me only a second to know I was still heading up, but I knew I couldn't make it alone. I had to convince a handful of the truly exceptional mountaineers who were attempting K2 that day to overcome their fear. Pleading for their assistance wouldn't have inspired confidence in them. I knew that I needed to lead by example. These were brave men. If they saw the summit as a possibility, it should be enough for them to push aside the probability of dying on K2.

Although Chris stumbled into this situation without warning, he was prepared for it. When Nima fell to his death, he knew he had to honor his soul and honor his friends before he could do anything else. To simply climb past them, ignoring their pain and suffering, would have turned the climb into a personal failure. When he accepted Nima's death, he broke through to a higher level of leadership and helped produce a historic event.

This ancient secret of embracing death unleashes the courage of your convictions as a high altitude leader, giving you power not available through any other path to take decisive action. The acceptance of failure, even death, as an option sets in motion a series of actions that counteracts the fear that paralyzes a group's collective goal.

**Accepting death is choosing life.
It grants us the power and freedom to act.**

History shows that leaders and companies that embrace death also achieve superior results. Suspend your disbelief in death as a management concept and you begin to see shadows of it everywhere:

- Near-death experiences can profoundly transform a person's life to take needed action. Why does a heart attack victim suddenly stop caring about the office politics that consumed his life before his near-death crisis and take new actions?

- Why did the famous Buckminster Fuller take the action to produce historic breakthroughs in mathematics, physics, and architecture only after he stepped back from the brink of suicide on the shore of Lake Michigan?

- The power of accepting death showed itself on 9/11 on Flight 93, en route from Newark to San Francisco. Initially the passengers probably behaved like those on the other fated flights that day, until somebody made a cell phone call. Then everything changed. When the hostages discovered the secret for power that al-Qaeda used, death, the passengers' power equaled that of the terrorists, and the passengers took action.

Although it has proven to work for centuries in taking leadership to higher altitudes in performance, embracing death remains a radical and unorthodox concept for many. Not everyone on your team or organization may be strong enough or brave enough to engage this process. Highly egocentric individuals will try to hide out, wait for it all to blow over, dismiss the process as worthless, or hope they won't be found out. These people ultimately will be exposed, just as weak climbers quit early in an expedition. But those in your organization who do embrace death successfully will never look back: embracing death allows decisive action in careers and organizations.

When we spoke with leaders about their most fearful experiences, the subject of death kept coming up. From a management point of view, this thing called death takes several forms; it doesn't have to be physical. Although our mountaineering teams face death in the most absolute sense, metaphorical death can also occur, from the boardroom to the production floor, and it can be just as transformative an experience. Leaders told us how embracing, versus avoiding or denying, the death of a goal, a project, a sale, or a career freed and inspired them to create new possibilities and actions.

Bankruptcy, the ultimate death of a company, enables companies to make great decisions they should have made much earlier, and perhaps avoided bankruptcy altogether. But until death was breathing down his or her neck, many managers were powerless to act in the face of their fears.

High altitude leaders find that these moments of imminent failure free them to take decisive action. The call to action from accepting such business deaths drives problem solving, decision making, and execution with greater clarity of vision. Suddenly a host of new possibilities exists, including ones they would have earlier dismissed. Acting in the face of death, not freezing up at the very thought of it, stops fear and allows you to continue climbing, pushing on past those paralyzed instead of giving up and descending. It isn't hard to find an entrepreneur who reminisces about gaining an entirely new level of ability after going flat broke or a professional who risked giving up her career to make a dream come true.

No better example of this paradox of fear and death is with former Vice Admiral Charles "Willy" Moore Jr. When Willy was deputy chief of naval operations for fleet readiness and logistics, he hired Don to help facilitate the strategy for transforming naval fleet readiness. Willy is a legend, although he'll never admit it. When he left the navy a few years ago after serving for over forty years, he was the most combat-experienced naval officer and the longest-serving naval pilot on active duty, an honored status in the navy known as a Grey Eagle. He had commanded naval squadrons and air wings twice, as well as a carrier strike group. Now he is vice president of global sustainment for Lockheed-Martin Aeronautics, a $12 billion business with thirty thousand employees. Willy is probably the best at understanding freeing yourself from fear by accepting death:

> My last combat operation was Operation Enduring Freedom. I slept like a baby. I never worried about anything. I flew into the combat zone, I walked the battlefield, and I was very, very comfortable the entire time. And it's a phenomenon that you know, Don, very well. In a military combat situation, you have already made a commitment to give up your life. You've made it consciously or unconsciously, but you made it. There's something very liberating about that. If this is it and it's my day to lose my life, then so be it.
>
> Not so in corporate work. Death in the business world is not necessarily physical death, but death of the ego. When we are too invested in our ego, we can't collaborate, change, adapt, and cooperate as a team. It's vital to be a team when there is a relentless pressure on revenue and having to change with market demands. If you can't accept death here, you're at a disadvantage. And it will kill you just as surely as in combat because your blood pressure rises, you put on weight, you stop sleeping, and the stress takes its toll. Then it's only a matter of time when you become another casualty.

Embracing the death of projects, goals, careers, teams, or companies frees leaders to create alternatives to becoming paralyzed and sliding off the cliff. In contrast, the normal response of seeking to deny death by clinging to cherished plans, opinions, or personal agendas can kill you metaphorically. Embracing death frees you to continue climbing.

If the genuine experience of having nothing left to lose opens up hitherto unimagined capacities, then what are you afraid of?

How to Die and Take Action

Strength is built through exercise. Here are a few exercises we learned as we stumbled and fell so many times through the valley of the shadow of death. These exercises inspire action in career development, team improvement, and executive leadership, even at altitudes below 26,000 feet.

Seek Fear

Seeking fear is critical. High altitude leaders purposely push themselves up against their limits on a regular basis. When Don first studied rock climbing, he remembers it like this:

> *Sewing machine leg.* That's what they called it. The fear of being a thousand feet up on a sheer rock face hanging on by your fingernails causes such fear that one of your legs starts shaking up and down, like you're running one of those old-time manual sewing machines. It's embarrassing, but you don't care; you're just trying to stay alive. Then, after you push through, you begin to trust your gear, your guides, and your capabilities. After a few days, you're leaning over the edge enjoying the view as if you're relaxing on your front porch.

You have to put yourself in fearful situations regularly in order to consistently overcome ever-larger fears. You don't have to take up rock climbing, but you do have to push your own limits. Maybe you are terrified of public speaking, or being criticized for your artistic talents, or swimming in deep water, or snakes. To practice doing scary stuff, start by addressing some of the issues within your life that you've been avoiding.

We like telling executives that no one wants to be led by a has-been. That really hits a lot of them in the gut. Here they are, business leaders who live in the comfortable world they built for themselves and surrounded by the trappings of success, and someone who has climbed an icy peak is insinuating that they've stopped being the leader they imagine themselves to be. We ask them, "How often do you take real risks in your career?" "Are you pushing your team to the limits of your industry?" "Are you exercising your strengths, so that when a crisis occurs you can act decisively?"

If you and your team aren't regularly pushing limits, you won't be able to overcome the life-or-death challenges that every person, every team, and every organization eventually faces. If you don't train, you won't reach the summit.

Kill Your Cherished Plans

High altitude leaders don't freeze when they fear the death of projects, ideas, and teams. Acting despite those real fears frees them to create alternatives.

In 1980 Don gained his first clue on this phenomenon at a business conference. A speaker revealed that in the 1950s, Lockheed's domination of the commercial aircraft market forced Boeing into a financially desperate situation. At a time when the entire industry was designed around propeller technology, Boeing had nothing left to lose. Accepting the inevitable gave it the freedom to kill its "propeller" dreams and risk putting a jet engine on a commercial airframe. It paid off. Lockheed, the number one player, withdrew from the market, and Boeing, en route to the summit, eventually ended up owning the second-place competitor, Douglas.

It doesn't take long to see the same pattern in hundreds of companies. Japan's threatening domination of the motorcycle market, for example, gave Harley-Davidson something to die for. There was no other choice. Harley-Davidson killed the processes it had invested so much in—fired consultants, let go of entrenched turf battles, and banded together in a desperate last stand to take back the market—and succeeded.

The Maryland Jockey Club, the oldest sports franchise in North America, is another example. The club was founded in 1743 and counts George Washington among its past customers. You probably know of its premier race: the Preakness Stakes of the Triple Crown, the world's most famous thoroughbred racing series. You might think that after surviving the American Revolution, the Civil War, Prohibition, World War I, the Great Depression, and World War II, this club would never die. The club had spawned such a large horse racing industry that in the 1980s, it accounted for more than seventy-five percent of the state of Maryland's total sports income (the combined gross revenues of professional football, professional baseball, professional basketball, professional hockey, and every other amateur and professional sport operating in the state).

But as the Maryland Jockey Club neared its 250th birthday, it almost ceased living. Frank DeFrancis, its inspirational CEO, had suffered a serious heart attack from which he would not recover. After he died, Frank's estate and his partners were faced with two enormous problems, both with the potential to be fatal. First, trying to replace Frank, who had almost single-handedly revived the company and led the Maryland horse industry into an era of unparalleled prosperity, was an enormous challenge. Second, the fundamental economics of the business were undergoing a paradigm shift of seismic proportions as a result of advancements in technology and major changes in the legal and regulatory structure that governed horse racing in the United States. Simulcast racing had arrived. Now people could bet on any horse race in America without even showing up at the track. Up to this point, bettors had to come to the track to bet, and the only races they could wager on were the ones run before their very eyes. The cash wagered was spent locally. But now the Maryland Jockey Club would be competing with Churchill Downs, Santa Anita, Belmont, Saratoga, and every other horse track in the country. Money wagered in Maryland would go to tracks and breeders thousands of miles away. How could the club possibly make a profit with this new business model?

Thousands of people were at risk of losing their jobs, and billions of dollars were at stake because of this twin set of corporate catastrophes: the untimely death of a charismatic leader and a radical shift in the industry. A new leader had to be found to fill Frank's gigantic shoes. But who would shoulder the burden of an organization that is about to die?

Three thousand miles away, Frank's son, Joe, was at the pinnacle of an incredibly successful career. He and his team had been hired by Kohlberg Kravis Roberts & Co. to serve as counsel to handle the antitrust aspects of the merger of RJR and Nabisco. At $25 billion, this was the largest leveraged buyout of all time. (This was the deal that made Michael Milken famous and was written about in the book and movie *Barbarians at the Gate*.)[3] Joe, thirty-four years old at the time, was perfectly positioned to be a key player in the growing, and insanely profitable, business of mergers and acquisitions.

Now, with his father dead, Joe was asked to give up his successful career to come back to Maryland to salvage the Maryland Jockey Club. If he saved the club, he would save his mother's and sister's long-term financial future and revitalize the important economic role that horse racing plays in Maryland; hundreds of small stables and farms employing thousands of trainers, breeders, stable hands, and jockeys would survive. If he failed, everyone would lose. Moreover, if he moved to the Jockey Club, he would lose his role at the peak of his legal career:

> I didn't waste too much time agonizing over the decision. I'd just been through the most grueling legal battle imaginable. I'd built a team and we won. That experience reinforced all I learned

about identifying risks and balancing them against the potential rewards. Yes, I had to take some great personal risks.

Stepping away from my legal career after that victory was a very risky proposition. The legal landscape was changing so quickly that my intellectual capital would soon be outdated. My contacts would dry up.

My path to partnership would be cut off. If I left now, I'd have to start from scratch if I needed to return to practicing law again. But my potential losses weren't nearly as great as the losses that threatened so many of the stakeholders. What options would a fifty-five-year-old horse trainer have if this industry failed?

It was pretty easy for me to weigh the risks and rewards and decide to return to Maryland. And once I made that decision, I didn't dare look back. It was full steam ahead.

Joe killed his legal career and returned to Maryland knowing that cherished traditions were about to be sacrificed. With so much at stake for the Maryland Jockey Club and Maryland's horse racing industry, Joe was just one of thousands of people who feared losing all they had in the fight ahead. But still he acted instead of freezing. It took a few years to rally thousands of stakeholders around a new customer-focused vision. But it allowed the 250-year-old Maryland Jockey Club to keep the best parts of its tradition, discard the limiting factors, and enter into the most prosperous years in its history.

Could you have sacrificed as much as Joe did to reach the summit?

Always Push Forward, but Do It Fast

In mountaineering, the beauty of pushing forward means that the higher your altitude, the farther you will see. At sea level, the horizon is just twelve miles away. On the summit of Everest, the horizon is twelve hundred miles away. When you can see that far, obstacles that once seemed impossible to overcome are put into perspective. The same happens when you push higher. So to achieve your full potential be sure to act when things get scary, and always be pushing forward. You certainly have met leaders who have this drive. No matter how deadly the climb may be, these leaders shoulder their load and continue climbing. They fight the immobilizing power of fear by acting. Joe DeFrancis didn't waste time agonizing over his decision to come to the aid of the Maryland Jockey Club. Chris didn't agonize over his decision to continue the K2 climb even after watching Nima Sherpa fall to his death.

In what areas of your life now have you just stopped? Why? What's it going to take to start pushing forward again? And why wait?

All the leaders we spoke with learned through brutal experiences how to act in spite of their fears, but they all impressed on us their wish that they had acted earlier in the process. In retrospect, they could see their organizations, or teams, or even themselves individually freezing. But by staying stopped for so long, they risked future success. Their teams slowly became less risk tolerant, emotions frayed, people withdrew, trust eroded, and they gradually lost strength. When everyone's best was needed, everyone had less to give. When teams or companies freeze, time relentlessly robs them of their potential to push forward again.

How long have you been stopped?

Just Remember Death

> One who is an executive must before all things keep
> constantly in mind, by day and by night, the fact
> that they have to die. That is his chief business.[4]

We've all dealt with the finality of death at some point. Maybe your business went bankrupt, your career fizzled out, you fired some employees, a great team drifted apart, your heart was broken, or your climbing partner fell for thousands of feet.

But have you noticed that very few cultures see death as the end? Most religions teach us that death is the beginning of something even better. Whether a better existence awaits, or one reincarnates to work through current failings, death is a door for what's next. And in business it's no different, as the many stories of people bouncing back from catastrophe to reach even bigger summits show. The proof exists: not every failure ends in disgrace. A lot of times, the consequence of failure is a previously unimaginable success.

So why do we fear failure and death so much? So many people are paralyzed by it. As leaders we avoid making difficult decisions because of this fear. Our teams suffer as a result and the very dream of reaching the summit ends in disappointment.

At Earth Treks, we had two charismatic and strong-willed employees running parts of the business that actually did not make much money, so keeping these employees around had a direct impact on our profits. The first guy left in disgrace: he stole our mailing lists and tried to cover it all up with a series of lies. In the end, he severed a relationship that was nearly a decade old. A year after he left, his department, properly managed, doubled in revenues and tripled in profits. The second guy left with dignity. He helped us sell his division to a competitor and went on to become the general manager of this new and larger company. Earth Treks was suddenly freed from the financial losses of that division. Every penny saved went directly to our bottom line.

It wasn't easy to admit that both of these situations were killing us. And even once we admitted it, it wasn't easy to act. Both times we delayed the inevitable course of action because we were afraid. But looking back, it's obvious that once we knew these things could kill us, we were freed to act. When we examine high altitude leaders, we learn that the very possibility of death frees them up to explore new possibilities.

Remembering the inevitability of death loosens the ego's grip.
Then honor, bravery, and integrity emerge in its place.
This is the secret to high altitude leadership.

Remembering death is easier if you're in a company that is dying. If not, congratulations. But an exercise you can do is to have a brutally honest discussion on what decisions and actions are being avoided because you don't have the necessary freedom and power to confront them. For example, if you're on a team, try the following at your next meeting:

1. Ask participants to ponder what they would do if the team, project, or company was dying.

2. Have everyone individually write down what they would do differently now that there's nothing left to lose—for example, what actions would be taken that previously had been avoided, what decisions would be made differently, which policies or processes would be changed, what resources would be managed differently.

3. Combine the common themes on a flip chart.

4. Challenge the group: "Why are we waiting?" Remember that not all ideas are good ones or make sense to act on because your team or project isn't dying, but can you really ignore everything on the list?

5. Develop actions to address the appropriate issues everyone has been avoiding.

6. Assign champions and time lines to the actions, and schedule a follow-up accountability session to check on progress.

Repeat this exercise at least a couple times per year.

Surviving a failure gives you more self-confidence. Failures are great learning tools—but they must be kept to a minimum.

Jeffrey Immelt, CEO of General Electric

Fail often in order to succeed sooner.

IDEO, a well-known, much-admired design firm

Fear Conquered?

You will never conquer all your fears, and you shouldn't want to. As we tell our mountaineering clients, fear focuses the mind. Every once in a while, we need to feel our hairs stand on end, our heart rate quicken, and our palms sweat. Without a little adrenaline, our lives would become boring and our team would stop focusing on its true goal.

Key Learnings

- Fear of death is natural, but freezing in the face of it paralyzes organizations and leaders.
- Acting decisively in the face of great fear triggers the actions needed for success.
- Embracing death provides freedom and power for innovation, decisiveness, and action.
- High altitude leaders don't cling to cherished projects, personal agendas, or career positions. They focus on strategic results.
- Act early. Waiting diminishes the chances for success.

Climbers nearing the summit of K2

2007 Shared Summits K2 Expedition, Bruce Normand

Danger #2

SELFISHNESS

Before the deed comes the thought.
Before the achievement comes the dream.
Every mountain we climb, we first climb in
our mind.

—*Royal Robbins, climber and entrepreneur*

K2, Summit Day, continued

4:30 P.M. Fifteen hours after leaving Camp 4, we finally reach K2's summit. Of the two dozen climbers who left the camp, only sixteen of us made it to the top. But it is too late in the day for us to enjoy this moment for long. Darkness can be seen on the eastern horizon. The sun is quickly setting. Soon the temperatures will plunge. We are still hours from the tents.

5:30 P.M. Descending into the mountain's shadow, we come upon two determined Italians still climbing upward. We are all surprised. I radio base camp, and their team there sounds equally shocked. Hours before, one of these climbers had been told to turn back, but they just kept going. When your ego drives you, the results are never pretty. They're committing one of the worst mistakes in mountaineering: summiting after the sun sets. I'm worried about the consequences this could have for all of us.

8:00 P.M. Thickening clouds hide the moon. We are descending through the darkest night I've ever seen. A few feet away, we hear a murmur but can't see where it is coming from. Lying in the snow, his light beneath his body, a Czech climber tries to call out, "Help me, I am dying." We pull him to his feet. He stumbles many times, his body now incapable of moving. He wants to sleep where he falls. He is ready to die. Exhausted, we wrap his arms over our shoulders and stagger to the tents. There is no one else to care for him, so we push him into our tent. We spend the night with four big men in a three-person tent. I give up my sleeping bag to keep the Czech alive.

9:30 P.M. The Italian team leader and I spot the lights of his two teammates on the traverse about a thousand feet above us. The climbers are descending slowly, but at least they are moving. It will be hours before they return to their tent.

11:30 P.M. One of the Italians finally calls on the radio. He can't find the tents and needs directions. He never mentions that he's alone, having left his slower partner to descend on his own. He has the pair's only radio. It appears he's looking out only for himself.

1:00 A.M. The lone Italian crawls into the group's tent at Camp 4. He tells the expedition leader that the last climber should arrive in a few minutes. They fall asleep.

3:00 A.M. One of the Italians conducts a brief and fruitless search (perhaps fifteen minutes) for the missing partner. The climbers fall back to sleep.

7:00 A.M. A Portuguese climber wakes us and the Italians. He alerts us that we need to get moving: a storm is approaching. He and his porter, along with the Russians and Koreans, start their descent at 7:30 as the full force of the storm hits the mountain.

8:20 A.M. Working with Czech climbers in base camp, we create an evacuation plan for their exhausted teammate. The Italians gather outside our tent, imploring us to guide them to

Camp 3. Unable to find the route, they are desperate for us to lead them to safety.

The Italian leader only then tells us that their last teammate never returned to the tents. We are shocked. How could they selfishly ignore his safety to get some sleep? We look outside the tent, but the life-threatening storm limits visibility to just a few yards. By not telling us until now, the Italians missed any opportunity for rescuing their fellow climber. Even finding our next destination, Camp 3, might prove impossible.

Selfishness kills people, profits, and possibilities. You already know this persistent danger that stalks organizations at every altitude. It doesn't take long to smell it coming. Take a sniff:

- Someone thinks of his career as he abandons the team.
- Critical problems remain covered up until there's no time left to resolve them.
- Turf wars are funded at costly expense to the company.
- Someone takes credit for another's idea.
- An employee tries hard to look good to the boss, even if it means making someone else look bad.

These may seem like innocent office politics, but selfishness brings down the largest of organizations. Postmortem business school case studies blame the failures on reasons like strategic missteps or poor implementation of good ideas. But digging deeper among the carcasses, we find that selfishness alone drove the denial, avoidance, blindness, or cover-ups until it was too late.

We met a somber group one morning at a Fortune 500 technology company. The company was on top of its game, featured in the business press as the leader in its industry. Here's the story we were told by a mid-Atlantic regional marketing staff member:

> Our team spent three sleepless nights developing the most accurate analysis of our market penetration. The results weren't impressive: our market share was eroding rapidly, and we needed to alert management so changes could be made. With the division vice president at our presentation next week, the time couldn't be better.
>
> To be safe, the regional manager wanted a preview of the presentation, and we were proud to show it to him. But instead of congratulating us, he yelled, "We can't show him this! It makes it look like we're losing in this region! Go back and get data that show progress."
>
> "But we *are* losing," someone on the team said.
>
> "It's all a matter of interpretation. I want him to think we're successful! I don't get bonuses on failing! Go back, and rework the numbers!" And he left the room abruptly.
>
> We were stunned and confused, and we looked at each other, not knowing what to do. Do we override our boss and tell the vice president the truth?
>
> Someone said, "I'm not going to tell the vice president. You tell him."
>
> Another said, "Not me! Career arrest! He'll retaliate if we make him look bad."
>
> We ended up altering the numbers, and it really sapped our morale.

The selfish "give me good news or I'll find somebody who can" culture drove the illusion of progress until the company fired half its workforce, starting with the CEO. They missed the competitive shift in the market. Selfishness made sure they never had a chance.

Let's look further into how selfishness damages teams.

Chris Warner climbing above Camp 3 on K2

2007 Shared Summits K2 Expedition, Bruce Normand

How Selfishness Hurts Us

K2, The Day After Reaching the Summit

8:30 A.M. We are packing up, each of us leaving the tent once we are ready. Outside, the three remaining Italians and an Iranian climber are desperately waiting to be led to the next lower camp. They are afraid that if they leave alone, they'll be lost in the storm or swept away by an avalanche. Their fear has them clinging to us. As we rush to strap on our crampons, we realize that one pair is missing from the front of the tent. The other pairs of crampons are neatly piled one atop the others, but the top pair is gone. It's a shocking and potentially fatal development. We spend nearly an hour searching, but they are gone. How could they just disappear? We can't help but think that a climber from another team must have lost his and so took ours. In disbelief, one of my partners, Don Bowie, is forced to descend the steep slopes without this vital piece of safety equipment.

11:30 A.M. Bowie is leading the stronger of the Italians and the Iranian. They are descending steep slopes and jumping crevasses in blizzard conditions. Just above Camp 3, he slips and falls for a hundred feet, tearing three ligaments in his leg. He must continue the descent in excruciating pain and with limited use of his left leg.

12:30 P.M. The Czech climber and I arrive at Camp 3. He looks too worn out to continue the descent. We crawl into a battered, but still standing, tent.

6:00 P.M. Exhausted and in pain, Bowie reaches a ten-foot gap in the ropes that he cannot traverse without crampons. He asks for help from another team. Someone responds with venom: "I am angry. I will not help you." Shocked, our partner watches the team pass him by. He waits for our last teammate, Bruce Normand, to arrive. When he gets there, Normand cuts a section of rope, and together they descend toward Camp 2.

8:00 P.M. Bowie finally arrives at Camp 2 and crawls into the three-person tent we were using, where some of our gear was stored. A few feet away, the battered Italian tent is being torn apart by the gale-force winds. Our tent is already crammed with the three Italians and the Iranian climber. One of the Italians, the same climber who abandoned his partner during the dark descent, is wrapped in our team's sleeping bag. When our injured climber asks to use it, the Italian replies: "Yesterday this was your sleeping bag. Tomorrow this will be your sleeping bag. But tonight this is my sleeping bag."

It is a sad commentary about mountaineers, but we constantly confront the issue of selfishness during mountain rescues. But appalling as it is, the problem of people simply turning their back on the needy extends beyond mountaineering. People selfishly protecting themselves above all else devours organizational performance everywhere.

Whenever we find selfishness in a company, it shows up in a destructive and unproductive condition, or what we call dangerous, unproductive, dysfunctional behavior (DUD). DUD behavior takes on a life of its own and frustrates even the best efforts of CEOs, managers, and employees.

What kinds exist? The list of DUD behaviors is endless: protection of sacred cow projects (continuing on long after they were told to turn back), blaming, avoiding accountability, back-stabbing, political maneuvering, CYA (a common vernacular for "cover your butt"), turf wars, silo protection, hidden agendas, taking credit for another's ideas, trashing other ideas to promote your own, withholding information, looking good to the boss, playing favorites, finger-pointing, power plays, passing the buck, gossiping, entitlement attitudes, and grin faking (smiling in agreement when you have absolutely no intention of supporting the project).

Regardless of industry, size, geography, or age, no company escapes a DUD infection. Yet many remain unaware of the threat. On our expeditions, clear risks of injury or death make detecting DUD damage easier and more important. One selfish act can kill a lot of people. In organizations, however, the damage often lies hidden. You'll never find it measured on the profit-and-loss statement, but selfishness lurks as the most dangerous blow to profitability. At The SAGA Leadership Institute, when we develop high-performance cultures in client companies, we get a close-up of how much selfishness damages an organization. Our conclusion:

Selfishness eats profits.

How much profit is lost? The results of analyzing over ten thousand executives from 1997 to 2007 are alarming: DUD behavior sucks 20 to 80 percent of productive time out of organizations, with the overall average hovering around 50 percent. People admit they waste half their time getting distracted by DUD behavior, yet rarely does a company measure this damage to productivity, quality, and speed. So when someone asks you how many people work at your company, chances are you should tell them, "About half."

Don't believe us? Look around. Ask your colleagues these questions:

- Ever had a fifteen-minute meeting take an hour?
- Ever see a project take twice as long as necessary?
- How often does someone say something outside the meeting that should have been said in the meeting?
- How many times has someone talked about someone else instead of challenging the individual directly?
- How many times have you been lied to or manipulated at work?
- How often have you been involved in a doomed project but no one says anything about the dismal chances for success?

We know that up to 5 percent of readers won't see a problem here. They're lucky and should keep doing what they're doing. The other 95 percent? There's still much more climbing left before you summit.

Damage from DUD extends beyond day-to-day productivity losses. Leaders find immeasurable costs occur from:

- Missed sales opportunities
- Quality erosion in products and services
- Higher legal exposure
- Lower sustainability of competitive advantage
- Increased waste

- Employee turnover
- Poor morale

The good news is that DUD behaviors provide more than enough material for Dilbert comics and new episodes of *The Office*. The bad news is that 50 percent is a lot of payroll to be throwing out the window.

DUD Behavior Cost Impact Analysis

The journey to higher altitude leadership requires investment and commitment. Is it worth doing at all? To find out, analyze the damage of doing nothing. At the next staff meeting, conduct the following exercise to determine how much DUD behavior is costing the company.

Have everyone write on a piece of paper what percentage of staff time is wasted on or distracted by dangerous, unproductive, dysfunctional behavior caused by selfishness. Use the list above to explain what types of behavior you're talking about.

Collect and calculate the data average of the group.

Next, take that percentage and calculate how much human capital waste is costing your organization annually using the following chart:

Human capital loss (insert your % wasted on DUD)	%
Annual payroll and benefits	× $
Annual opportunities lost (for example, missed sales, higher waste, poorer quality, rework)	+ $
Increased risk (for example, legal fees, insurances, workers' compensation, employee lawsuits)	+ $
Total annual cost to company	$

How much is DUD behavior hurting your company? Is it enough to care about?

If selfishness eats profits, then why don't managers immediately fix the problem? How come it gets so bad before anything is done? To be fair, many leaders try to fix the problem. They hire trainers, coaches, consultants, motivational speakers, and other services. But the failure rates of these interventions are high because they miss the target; they don't address the root cause.

The Root of Selfishness

Scenes like this create cynicism among experienced managers and employees:

> "I don't know what else to do," said the human resource manager of a large manufacturing company. "We've just completed another training series to help get rid of the silo mentality and selfish politics around here, but nothing seems to have any lasting effect."
>
> "Did you know that the failure rate data on these types of training programs range from 70 to 100 percent depending on the study?" I asked.
>
> She fell back in her chair. "They failed to mention that when they sold me the program."
>
> Realizing that her experience was normal didn't help diminish her feeling that she had been duped.

Repeated efforts to improve the culture and performance of companies with organizational change interventions continually fall short. At best, DUD behavior goes underground for a little while, then reemerges only weeks after the experts leave. Why the high failure rates?

Seeking the cause of training and consulting program failures drove our early research. The answer eventually came from an unlikely place: not management journals or motivational speakers but from the laboratory. By studying the work of exceptional scientific researchers, we found that we all were being duped. Popular change program theories address just the symptoms, not the root cause, of the problem: human selfishness. DUD behaviors fail to be trained out of an organization as industry experts think because the real root of selfishness ends up being biological, not cultural. It's a natural, fear-based instinct programmed into our species to ensure genetic survival. Scientists have concluded that selfish strategies are the most effective for species evolution.[1] In

> *Genetic animal instincts drive our relationships more than we ever knew. It's not politically correct, but it's scientifically accurate.*
>
> Dr. Pat Allen, *psychotherapist*

the real world of evolution, any animal thinking this is a warm, cooperative universe where we could just talk things out and have a group hug eventually becomes a food product for another species.

On mountains and in companies, this primal agenda gets in our way. It robs us of leadership power and usurps the freedom needed for producing great results. Employees naturally perceive a world of threat or fear in a company. Whether the threat is real or not, it still exists because that's what humans are supposed to perceive. Today this human biological drive collides with the needs of modern organizations, bleeding profits and sending many companies off the cliff. How many times do selfish employees hoard or steal resources, ignore another in need of help, or fight to preserve their self-image at the expense of the organization? This selfish drive won't change anytime soon, and it pokes its head into a company whenever an employee thinks:

"I can't afford to be seen as wrong or weak."

"I want that under *my* control, not someone else's."

"Am I being outmaneuvered or manipulated?"

"Will I be found out?"

Successful diminishing of DUD behaviors in an organization requires unhooking this biological agenda. Only then can leaders deal more authentically with the issues and problems and bring forth bravery, clarity, and transformation. Ignoring this agenda only wastes more money on training and consulting change programs. As evolutionary psychologist Dr. Pat Allen was guiding our genetic research, she told me one day, "No matter how culturally sophisticated we think we are, our biology will not be ignored."

Luckily this biological selfish drive can be unhooked. Leaders salvage botched organizational development programs and move people from genetic survival to organizational success by using an ancient secret: a compelling saga.

SURVIVAL TIP: A Compelling Saga

How do leaders create and sustain greatness in spite of the selfish human program that pushes every leadership theory off the cliff during implementation? We struggled with this question for a long time. We read all the popular leadership books, listened to the best motivational speakers, and followed the methods of the top consulting firms.

They were of no help.

All that changed when we noticed that our Himalayan expeditions seemed to falter at the end of the journey, not the beginning. For example, on one expedition, Don's team had to cross many 17,000-foot-high passes to get to the villages and monasteries they were exploring. We continuously learn from visiting remote cultures as part of our research, but on this particular trip, Don learned more from the Americans on the team. It happened at the end of the expedition, on the way back to civilization. After almost a month in the mountains, Don noticed the American team leader looking a little depressed. He was always pumping the team up but now seemed tired and removed. Concerned, Don asked him how he was feeling.

"I'm fine. I just hate this part of every expedition I lead," he said.

"What do you mean? This part?"

"Well, most expedition teams fail on the way down, not the way up."

"But we're fine. We had a couple medical emergencies, and they were handled," Don said, confused.

"No, I'm not talking about that. I'm talking about the group. Just look around. It's not a collaborative, supporting team anymore. There's no more passion. Everybody's cliquing up into their own little factions, and they're starting to complain and whine about everything," he said.

He was right. The group had degraded from a high-performance team to one resembling the apathetic conditions we see in companies. What happened to the team? The answer was simple: there was no next pass ahead. Without a challenge before them, everyone started putting personal desires ahead of the group's goals and reverting to their own selfish behaviors.

Human selfishness can only be unhooked when a greater passion overwhelms the selfish agenda.

Can it be that simple? Is purging the selfishness that sabotages performance all about managing a greater shared passion? We validated this in the world's oldest organization: military operations. When our work was making the rounds at the Pentagon, we were asked to tour military operations with a small group as a guest of the secretary of defense. "We'll show you what CNN doesn't get to see, and you have permission to ask anybody, anything, at any time," they told us.

We jumped at the chance for this research opportunity. What we found was remarkable: the importance of passion permeated the leadership approach of all the generals and admirals, much more so than the leaders we saw in corporations. Military training remains clear on this point: higher-morale troops win more battles than demoralized troops, and sometimes in spite of a weaponry disadvantage. Why do you think leaders always ask how the moral is before battle? Whether you're commanding an army, summiting a mountain, or leading a team, passion is the critical factor.

Passion, we found out later, is also an ancient management insight. Throughout history, great leaders constantly focused on creating passion in their people by inventing stories of gods, kings, and heroes. The ancient Norse called it a saga, and leaders for millennia knew the art of conceiving one. High altitude leaders throughout history knew that compelling sagas effectively inspire passion and give people something worth fighting for. The compelling saga leverages the leader's power in aligning people toward a higher cause than the agenda of their ego.

Humans need a compelling saga:
a story or drama that inspires passion for a strategic result,
a passion that overwhelms the selfishness common in humans.

A compelling saga possesses some or all of these dimensions:

- Has a dramatic theme to beat an enemy target, achieve an ideal, or fulfill a purpose
- Sets a goal that's difficult to achieve, a challenging summit that needs to be conquered
- Is captured in language that drives performance, values, and strategic focus even in the face of risk, sacrifice, or pain
- Sets the context of how success (or failure) will be defined
- Focuses people on strategic results, not selfish, territorial, gossipy, soap operas
- Although a brief statement, spawns stories and legends that permeate an organization's culture

Today's companies no longer teach these stories. Instead they create a vision, mission, values, and a strategy, but these elements typically fail to inspire the passion needed to achieve the strategic result (see Figure 2.1). A few do but many turn out to be passionless platitudes that forget to provide the background for the struggle and pain, the triumph and sacrifice. They explain the business but fall short in giving people something to "die" for—to subjugate their selfishness to. Managers dutifully document these elements because the books say organizations need them. But the result ends up being empty content hanging on walls, printed on business cards, or woven into the corporate lexicon.

Because missions and visions typically appear as perfunctory descriptions and not a saga, employees abandon their mission statements at the first sign of distress—if, that is, they believed in them at all. The ensuing passionless vacuum that remains gets filled by the employees with their own selfish, petty dramas. But why can't employees live with descriptive missions and visions?

After leading over 150 international mountaineering expeditions and consulting with over 7,500 CEOs, the two of us find one thing is most common: humans crave sagas in the truest sense of the word. They seek tales of epic proportions that teach a universal lesson. Given the chance to participate in an epic journey, many people are inexplicably pulled toward it. Given the chance to climb Everest, people train for years, mortgage their homes, and all too often forsake common sense as they push ever upward, just like entrepreneurs.

People's innate desire to achieve something significant while they are on this earth explains the attraction of sagas. Examples show up all around us. In his book, *Man's Search for Meaning*, Victor Frankel writes how concentration camp prisoners who had something significant left to do had higher survival rates.[2] Those who did not died early. POWs often share the same story: healthy prisoners who feel as if they have nothing to live for fade fastest. In survival situations, people with a positive mental attitude and something or someone else to live for are more likely to survive.

Similarly, many CEOs admit that passion alone kept their company alive in the darkest of situations. That passion wasn't born from some planning session but from the personal will to survive and insights on how to win the game (for example, "if we band together, we will be much stronger than if we fight alone")—a compelling saga inspired by the threats. We found similar stories in all high altitude cultures:

- When Joe DeFrancis was fighting to keep the Maryland Jockey Club alive, he made one question central in every conversation: "What do our customers want?" With this framing of the conversations, it became harder for entrenched stakeholders to place their needs ahead of the group's goal.

- Don met a CEO who was on the board of Federal Express and exclaimed that the board meeting agendas must be pretty intense.
  "No, not at all," was the CEO's response.
  "Why not?" Don asked.
  "Well, we only ask one question."
  "Which is?"
  "What was late?" the CEO said.

- Another CEO who does business with Southwest Airlines said that when he walked into the airline's management offices, they basically said, "If what you want to talk about doesn't make us faster or cheaper, we don't have time to chat."

Compelling sagas help focus the questions. They bring the vision, mission, values, and strategy to life. Sagas capture the epic challenge in what some have called a rallying cry or battle charge, and they provide that emotional trigger to focus on a cause that makes our selfish agendas seem trivial.

Why aren't compelling sagas used more often? Two reasons commonly show up:

- Industry experts earnestly promote the positive, touchy-feely, optimistic statements and shy away from the ugly, uncomfortable, and even painful elements of the epic journey. Yet it is precisely the epic journeys that drive passion.

- One team's or company's compelling saga may not inspire passion in another. In an age where copying quick-fix ideas is common, few companies take the time to craft their own saga. They don't realize that the journey to peak performance remains personal to the group and can't be copied.

Figure 2.1 How a Compelling Saga Complements Common Business Concepts

Mission or Purpose

(Who are we? Why are we in business?)

|

Vision

(Where are we going?

What is the visual picture of our success at some point in the future?)

|

Values

(What drives our behavior?)

|

Strategy

(How do we achieve the vision? How do we win?)

|

Compelling Saga

(What language inspires our passion for the strategic result?

Why should we die—submit our ego—for the mission, vision, and strategy?)

If we look at successful contemporary organizations over the past century we see signs of a compelling saga in their language. The following examples were used when these companies were in their early stages or in new market initiatives:[3]

Early Compelling Saga Examples

Wal-Mart: Give ordinary folks the chance to buy the same things as rich people.

Mary Kay: Provide unlimited opportunity to women.

Honda: We will destroy Yamaha!

Nike: To experience the emotion of competition, winning, and crushing competitors. Nike's saga today is, "Bring inspiration and innovation to every athlete in the world." It does.

HP: To make technical contributions for the advancement and welfare of humanity.

Komatsu: Encircle Caterpillar.

Lexus: Beat Benz.

Citicorp: Become the most powerful, the most serviceable, the most far-reaching world financial institution that has ever been.

Coke: Put Coke within arm's reach.

Boeing: Bring the commercial world into the jet age.

FedEx: Beat the "brown shirts" with our red, white, and blue trucks.

Harley-Davison: Fulfill dreams through the experience of motorcycling.

What compelling saga drives your company right now? Your team? Your career? Passions that align people toward high-performance behavior drive the greatest achievements in careers and companies. A compelling saga captures this strategic drama and draws in masses of people. But how do you implement one?

How to Implement a Compelling Saga

In climbing, compelling sagas don't occur as often as they should, even though most of the formula exists in the sport. We have an obvious goal (the mountain), determined characters possessing incredible skill (the climbers), and challenges of the three main literary types: people versus nature, people versus people, and people versus themselves. What we might not have is the language to inspire passion for a winning strategy with clearly defined values and the courage of our convictions. When we do, it makes all the difference.

On K2, the Italian team split up, leaving a member to die on the mountain. Their selfish ego was running the agenda. Contrast this to our team, which brought our injured climber and the near-death Czech climber safely home. When people were dying, our gear was stolen, our teammate was injured, the blizzard was blowing, our tent was hijacked, and we were hungry and tired. But our K2 team still acted altruistically because we had a compelling saga. Our stated strategy and shared common values weighted the priorities clearly: safety, summit, style—and exactly in that order.

Chris remembers it this way:

> The most important thing was for all of us to survive the expedition. K2 had killed sixty-four people in the years leading up to our climb. One in seven summiters dies descending from the top. Two more climbers died on this summit push. We knew that if we were all to live, it was because our first priority was to fight to keep each other alive. We also desperately wanted to reach the top. This was my third expedition to the mountain. It defeated both of my earlier teams, just as it defeats most other teams that attempt it. In five of the past ten years, K2 has kept every team from its summit, and even in a successful year, summits come with a price. In 2006, four people summited, but six other climbers were killed. We also had our professional

reputations at stake. We were filming this expedition for NBC, and a mountaineering documentary that ends without a summit will never be shown. Finally, we were consumed by this concept of style. Mountaineering has grown into a sport that is judged more by whether you reach the top, without concern to how you go there.

As purists we set out to climb K2 in the most adventurous way we could. We set off to climb a remote, previously unclimbed face as a small team, without the help of Sherpas or bottled oxygen. Our plan was extremely ambitious and risky, and in the end we didn't reach the highest ideals of this goal. We failed on two new routes. Forty-five days into the expedition, we switched routes to a ridgeline occupied by six other teams. It was a blow to our morale, but after a few days of pouting, we accepted this new reality and fought for the summit with all of our original enthusiasm. In the end, as the epic ascent and descent unfolded, who would argue that our actions weren't in the best tradition of the sport? Our compelling saga got us through it all.

Here's how you can create your own compelling saga for your team.

Step 1: Prepare for Crafting

Crafting is an art. Seeing it as anything else quickly becomes a dead end. Your saga might appear solid in your mind when you wake up in the morning, but usually it needs to be crafted and recrafted to get it right. It can't be copied from another team. Compelling sagas emerge from a confluence of your team's winning strategy, cultural fit, leadership style, personal passion, and a host of other elements. A compelling saga is felt in the soul. It fills you with a mixture of anxiety and enthusiasm. Whether you're crafting a saga for your company, your team, or your own professional career, if you expect a logical and predictable process, stay in step 1 until you get over it.

Step 2: Base It on a Winning Strategy

A compelling saga should capture the essence of the winning intention of the mission, vision, values, and strategies of the team or company. The last thing you want is someone getting passionate about something that makes no sense for business performance. For example, although Data General, Braniff Airlines, Enron, and DEC had passion, their sagas were ill focused.

In fact, most teams or companies don't even have a strategy. They may have a tactical plan with a strategic planning cover, but it's not a strategy. Worse, the majority of strategic plans never get executed, and most of those that are executed fail to achieve the expected results.

You want a strategy that defines winning. High altitude leaders then take the strategy and craft the language that inspires passion for the challenge ahead—the compelling saga. This can be especially challenging when profits are slipping, employee morale is low, and competition is fierce. But history shows that high altitude leaders excel during apparently hopeless and impossible times; they find the passion to excel in the face of daunting challenges.

Step 3: Make It Memorable

Some companies or teams create compelling sagas that are too complicated and lengthy. Keep it simple and short so that it can be remembered easily.

Step 4: Always Be Vigilant

High altitude leaders are always on guard against DUD sabotage. They watch and listen to their people constantly. Review the clues from earlier in this chapter, and make your own list for DUD hot spots in your culture—for example, How often does a manager take credit for another's successful ideas? Do people tend to shift blame for failures versus assuming responsibility? Ensure your team detects DUD behavior early.

Step 5: Go Back to Step 1

Winds change, routes become impossible, and a fresh layer of snow turns a gentle slope into an avalanche trap. Keep crafting.

Don't ever forget that you're creating a compelling saga because if you don't craft the drama first, your team will likely fill that drama void with its own petty dramas. Using the aligned passion of a team helps fight the very selfishness that causes DUD behaviors that kill teams.

You now know how to survive the dangers of fear of death and selfishness, but there are still demons ahead. The next one seduces you into thinking your structures, processes, systems, and even the content you've learned here are actually important. Prepare for the danger of tool seduction.

Key Learnings

- Selfish DUD behavior eats profits while making work less satisfying.
- The source of DUD behavior lies not in human culture but in human biology. Ignoring this weakens training programs, cultural change, and vision and mission statements.
- Unhooking this selfishness happens not from motivational speeches but from crafting a compelling saga: language and actions that inspire passion for a strategic result.
- The compelling saga drives performance, inspires value-based behavior, and provides strategic focus.
- Sagas must be crafted, not copied, and may even evolve over time.

Mount Cho Oyu (26,908 feet), seen from advanced base camp

Chris Warner

Danger #3

TOOL SEDUCTION

My advice for climbers is to really tune into your
own passions and not just what other people are
doing or aren't doing.
Figure out what works for you, what turns you on,
what gives you the greatest amount of energy and
feeling of satisfaction.
> —*Galen Rowell, climber and photographer*

With the best equipment in the world the man with
poor judgment is in mortal danger.
> —*Royal Robbins, climber and entrepreneur*

Location: Cho Oyu, Tibet—The World's Sixth-Tallest Mountain

After guiding Everest expeditions and summiting even more
threatening mountains like K2, climbers get used to the moods
of the Himalayas. Some moods are predictable, especially the
cantankerous grumblings of the monsoon. The monsoon crashes
into the Himalayas each June. It's so powerful that the jet stream,
a belt of 200 mph winds encircling the earth, is pushed north past
the summits of the Himalayas. In mid-September, the monsoon
slowly fades away, and in that narrow band of calm weather
between monsoon-fed blizzards and the jet stream hurricane
lies the opportunity to summit. In September 1999, nearly four
hundred mountaineers gathered at the base of Cho Oyu, at
26,908 feet, the world's sixth-tallest mountain. To get to the base
of the mountain requires a journey across the Tibetan plateau.

Yet this pilgrimage takes place every year, mainly because Cho Oyu is among the "easiest" of the world's tallest peaks.

Cho Oyu has become such a popular mountain that the same level of infrastructure that is built on Everest is applied to climbs on this peak. Large commercial expeditions, employing dozens of Sherpas, set up a well-stocked base camp and three smaller but also well-supplied camps on the mountain. Thousands of feet of rope are strung between the camps, simplifying the commute. Each tent is equipped like a hotel room, outfitted with sleeping bags, mini-stoves, bags of food, and bottles of oxygen. Clients travel from camp to camp with day packs slung over their shoulders. Climbing Cho Oyu, or Everest, or any of the world's other tallest peaks in this manner is significantly less challenging than attacking the mountain as a small team as we were doing without the help of Sherpas and all the convenient tools of the trade.

My partner and I were the first to reach base camp. A day later, a large commercial expedition arrived. Our solitude was shattered, as we expected, so we moved higher. Again and again, we established our camps first, only to have tents sprout up all around us. Carrying less gear and needing less infrastructure, we made quick progress. The large teams lagged behind because their gear was so much more extensive.

In mid-September that year, something unusual happened: the monsoon lurched back to the north. At that moment, we sat in our tent at 23,000 feet while the closest team camped a few thousand feet below us. The snowstorm hit so quickly and with so much force that five inches fell the first hour and even more the second. We had no choice but to pack up and run for base camp.

Two hundred feet below camp, a crack shot across the slope I was crossing. The crack became an avalanche, the snow rushing past my legs like water in a river. Curious, I watched the snow slide past me. Engrossed in the excitement of this little slide, I never imagined that my cute little avalanche could become so deadly. This slide actually triggered a three-hundred-acre slope above, causing a massive avalanche that raced toward me.

I never heard it coming.

I never saw it coming.

I just remember standing on this small slope, watching the snow swoosh over my feet and push against my calves, when suddenly a silent wave of snow, ten feet high, picked me up. Pure whiteness and complete silence engulfed me. I tumbled deeply inside this tidal wave, flipping and spinning like a white sock among white sheets in an arctic clothes dryer.

The avalanche finally spit me to the side into the slower-moving snow at its edge, burying me to my neck and then, free of me, it plunged over a 300-foot cliff band.

My partner, above me as I disappeared, was astonished to find me alive. Our expedition didn't end with that close call, but 90 percent of the other climbers attempting Cho Oyu that season should have taken it as an omen. They would have saved themselves a lot of heartache and backaches if they just packed it in that day. Instead we all waited for the storm cycle to play itself out, which it eventually did. Precious time was wasted, though, because the Sherpas needed to move even more gear into place. Ten days later, the big groups were no farther along. And when the tiny window finally opened, a small handful of us, those not needing all sorts of tools and comforts, snuck to the summit. The largest groups watched hopelessly from base camp.

The season closed with a massive storm surge, killing nearly thirty climbers across the Himalayas and ending dozens of expeditions, whole camps buried by meters of snow. It was one of the most disastrous seasons in years. On Cho Oyu, 90 percent of the climbers, with an impressive display of the finest climbing tools, failed to reach the summit.

You want to have the best tools of leadership. And there are so many of them out there. Thousands of books, trainers, and experts teach how to use them—tools like the best way to structure a team, motivate others, make great decisions, influence, serve, plan, inspire, set values, gain respect, take initiative, empower, achieve goals—and get people to follow you to the summit.

The two of us don't feel like experts because we're still learning about leadership ourselves. But after leading over 150 international mountaineering expeditions and working with over seven thousand CEOs, we did learn one thing, and learned it the hard way. The best advice we can give you is simply this: Stop! You're going in the wrong direction.

The answer does not lie in the tools. In mountaineering, an overdependence on Sherpas, tools, and infrastructure can limit talented climbers. Similarly, a parade of consultants packing the latest tools and theories can bog down progress and distract companies from focusing on the vital issues.

Of course, tools are important. Before we climb up to the death zone, we spend a lot of time testing gear and perfecting skills. Managers do the same thing. (Only a fool would do otherwise.) But in critical moments, even the best tools break or fail in some other way, resources are lost, or circumstances counted on fail to materialize—yet still you must survive. The problem isn't with the tools; it's in how you relate to them. Do the tools support your success, or are they just an industry fashion trend? Do they allow you to act in the face of your fears, or do they just clog your shelves with interesting but irrelevant information? Do they fuel your team's passion for the challenge ahead, or do they derail production with useless meetings, lingo, and processes?

Are you using the tools, or are they using you?

If the latter, you can hear the warnings echoing throughout the halls:

**Incoming program-of-the-week!
Keep your heads down!**

And the stories are always the same:

- "I couldn't believe it! They were implementing Total Quality Management in our R&D department. We do research! I mean, it took the wind right out of us. We weren't even sure if we could creatively interact with each other unless it was a 'quality' conversation. Would our innovative thoughts be of insufficient quality? The classes were a waste of time. It was ridiculous."
- "Why did we have to waste so much time on Six Sigma? I mean we were only making bottle caps. They worked great at Three Sigma!"
- "When they hired a large consulting firm to implement matrix management, we thought it would help us become more effective. But the resulting power plays and leadership collisions at the top almost brought the organization to its knees."
- "We still haven't recovered from the cultural damage of our latest reengineering effort."
- "When our boss read about participative management, he just abdicated everything. We were directionless. I know he was trying to improve his leadership, but it caused six months of productivity losses before he got back in the game."

Do organizational change models, leadership theories, and other pop management fashion trends suck productivity and morale out of your organization? If they do, you are not alone. Imagine our shock, a scientist and a mountain climber, when we were exploring the management consulting industry. Our initiation was unsettling. At an international meeting of the world's top consultants, Mike Beer from Harvard Business School presented a paper on his research, "Why Change Programs Don't Produce Change," in which he declared that all large-scale organizational changes fail.[1]

We began researching other studies on the high implementation failure rates of leadership theories. Apparently Mike Beer was not alone. Studies of the billions of dollars spent on quality improvement, team building, reengineering, ropes courses, culture change, and various training and development programs showed failure rates well over 70 percent. Although the theories worked in many of the cases mentioned in the books, replication into other companies failed miserably.

One thing shocked us more: none of the world's experts challenged the failure data of their theories. And the data still remain mysteriously missing from their consulting brochures.

This piqued our curiosity.

Later we found that we had stumbled onto nothing new. These shocking insights were old and deeply felt in one particularly large group of people: employees. Apparently employees always see the problems with trendy management theories, and they don't need rigorous academic research to prove they are right. They instinctively sense the disaster coming when the lights are on, the chairs are filled, and the CEO announces the next big change program for the organization. Next, classes are scheduled, experts cruise the halls, and new processes, policies, and systems are introduced. Sooner or later the posters come down, the coffee cups with the new mottos sit unused on shelves, and the experts go home. Employees become more demoralized and cynical as piles of dead theories, training workbooks, and management consultant invoices grow ever higher.

Such cynicism drove even more research. What was being done to fix this problem? Surely the management consulting and training industries (being hounded by journalists and academics for producing unimpressive results for over $100 billion invested yearly) would desperately be fixing the problem. To our surprise, no one was seeking a remedy. Instead, they were seeking excuses. And there were as many excuses as there were failures:

- Client did not have enough training.
- Client had weak corporate culture.
- Client wasn't committed.
- Client had bad management.
- Client executed poorly.
- Client didn't follow through.
- Client was stupid.

And there were a hundred others.

But these issues are all predictable and measurable. Why were such clients engaged at all if they had these problems? Just as in mountaineering expeditions, we discovered the hidden source of the problem: tool seduction.

Why Tool Seduction Happens

Tools offer hope, and they make people feel that they have the right answer. After all, people are rewarded their whole life for knowing the right answer. But a problem occurs when employees use tools as crutches for safe answers. Who dares to argue with the ideas from a best-selling business book? Knowing the lingo and believing the authors actually implemented the idea themselves makes you look really, really good. But the results aren't pretty when you get seduced by best-selling ideas, buzzwords, and cool concepts. Tool seduction is costly and risky.

The risks of tool seduction can be seen every time a group of climbers dresses in the latest gear but applies the wrong techniques to the challenge at hand. In their overconfidence (or naiveté), they end up lost on a storm-ravaged slope for days while experienced climbers are at base camp having a beer and watching the weather.

How do we prevent new climbers from falling into tool seduction? *We tell them to stop reading mountaineering books.*

Why? Because those books have one of the following two effects on the uninitiated:

- They delude people into thinking that they are better than they are.
- They fill climbers with anxiety.

Either way leads to failure.

Perhaps the same advice should be used by today's companies. Both dead climbers and bankrupt companies are found grasping great tools. And the consulting industry doesn't help matters. They get paid for selling more tools, even though most of the management ideas have never been tested. For example, as a favor to a client, Don once helped an author from one of the top three consulting firms write an introduction to his new book. He was having trouble finding the right words to pull the reader in. Don suggested he use examples of successful applications of the book's theories to stimulate the reader's interest. The author looked at Don as if he were a dimwit and said, "We haven't applied any of these methods. There're no data to share about success rates." This was not this author's first book, and it probably won't be his last. Don left the room, not knowing whether to laugh or cry.

Maybe consultants should take the same pledge as doctors: *Primum non nocere* (first, do no harm).

How to Detect Tool Seduction

To determine if tool seduction has infected your organization, first consider whether you have enough tools already. When we work with clients to help them improve their strategy, executive team leadership strength, market positioning, or cultural alignment, we find that most of them already have plenty of tools. Think about it. Is the problem in your organization that you have a deficiency of these tools?:

- Goals and plans?
- Meetings?
- E-mails?
- Team-building programs?
- Process improvement programs?
- Quality initiatives?
- Did we mention meetings?
- [insert latest management trend here]

Chances are you too have enough (and maybe too many) of these things. Tool seduction is happening in your organization if one or more of the following exists. (We warn you not to be too fascinated with these detection methods lest you get seduced into another tool seduction.)

Cultural Artifacts

Assess your organizational culture for clues. You probably have tool seduction if:

- Managers keep throwing tools at a problem hoping it goes away as they continuously seek the next great theory to solve organizational woes.
- The CEO hires a consultant to uncover what everyone already knows instead of pointing out the painful reality himself or herself.
- Managers brag about which author they saw at the last conference or who they "personally" know.
- The staff uses buzzwords to make themselves look good in front of their peers.
- The staff uses the latest lingo or change programs to make someone else look stupid or further their own personal agenda. When consulting with a Fortune 10 company,

Don was stunned when a vice president said to another peer, "Watch out, or I'll use you as a bad example in my next training program."

Change Program of the Week

Is your staff whiplashed from frequent change programs? Or is the company championing yet another change program even though the previous thirty failed miserably? We at The SAGA Leadership Institute commonly find train wrecks from multiple failed change programs at client companies. Fixing all the damage certainly helps fund future institute research, but we can't help but feel the damage could've been avoided.

Company Size

Larger companies can be more susceptible than smaller ones to tool seduction. As more layers in the organization are formed, people become more and more distanced from the customer. Often cultures evolve where political power replaces bottom-line performance results. The more levels of bureaucracy that exist between customers and senior management, the more tool seduction threatens the organization.

Has the world you invented replaced the real world?

Fascination with Formal Plans

Having a plan isn't bad. In fact, it's a great tool. But even the most experienced climbers and managers are seduced with the illusion that the plan is progress itself. Often the plan takes on a life of its own, and when that happens, it becomes a dangerous tool, precluding adaptation. Adaptation is vital because no plan survives its impact with reality.

In mountaineering we call this reality of avalanches, sudden storms, rockfall, and other abrupt changes *objective dangers*.

Ignoring them spells catastrophe in expeditions. In the blink of an eye, everything can change. The most finely tuned visions and carefully planned strategies are destroyed. "Men plan, God laughs," the saying goes. Just as unsuspecting climbers are swept away by objective dangers, managers are swept away in these situations:

- The competitive landscape suddenly changes.
- Market conditions fall.
- Rivals outmaneuver your route.
- Competitive assumptions fail to materialize.
- Regulatory winds change.
- Economic rock slides happen.
- Customer demands shift.
- Resources become constrained.

The U.S. Army teaches all of its young officers a simple eight-step formula, called the troop leadership procedure:[2]

1. Receive the mission.
2. Issue the warning order.
3. Make a tentative plan.
4. Start necessary movement.
5. Reconnoiter.
6. Complete the plan.
7. Issue the complete order.
8. Supervise.

The emphasis on action shows the beauty of this system: you don't complete the plan until you've started the necessary movement and reconnoitered the battlefield.

Chris found an objective danger in the mail on Christmas Eve 2007: the State of Maryland delivered a notice stating that corporate income taxes had been increased by 18 percent, and sales taxes went up by 20 percent. For business owners like Chris, who has a retail department and pays income taxes, this was a government-triggered rockfall with what he called a big "lump of coal landing right in our stockings."

SURVIVAL TIP: Behavior and Adaptation

Location: Mount Shivling, India

Two friends and I barely survived two days trapped on a table-sized ledge more than halfway up an 8,000-foot, ice-plastered granite face in the Indian Himalayas. We had no tent for shelter and no way to melt snow for water or to cook a meal. Our planned strategy for ascent was thwarted as winds increased so high that they almost pried us from the ledge. Snow piled up over our bodies. Avalanches roared past. Blasts of air pushed the snow deep into our sleeping bags. Encased in ice, between layers of frozen feathers and light nylon, we couldn't even hear each other yell.

Finally, the snow stopped, but the clouds promised another blizzard. If we were to take advantage of this brief window and survive, we had to adapt our strategy to these new circumstances—and do it at once. If we tried to descend by the route we came up, we'd be killed by the avalanches. The only hope was to climb up for thousands of feet and then descend on an unseen side of the mountain.

As we left the relative security of our tiny ledge, we were unprepared for what became a three-day journey. Our fight for survival grew in complexity. The only pot we had for melting snow for hydration and cooking was torn away by a fierce wind. We had to adapt a foil windscreen into a makeshift pot that held only a few ounces of water. For food, we survived on a single Twix bar each day.

Remember two things:

- Behavior, not tools, drives results.
- Adapt or die.

It wasn't the tools that saved us in the Himalayas that time; we lacked or had lost them. Rather, our behavior—the decisions and actions we took—ensured our survival. If we hadn't adapted and readapted our plans, death would have been imminent.

High altitude leaders survive the danger of tool seduction by driving results from a behavioral perspective. Focusing on behavior and adaptation like appropriate decisions, actions, deeds, and conduct replaces tool seduction on mountains and in companies.

Regardless of how much you spend on books, training, experts, and meetings, it's all a waste if behavior doesn't change so that people start making different decisions and taking different actions. Most of the problems you're having in your organization are behavioral, not tool based. Someone is either doing something unproductive or using tools the wrong way. You can equip a climber or manager with the finest gear and hours of training, but without the correct behavior, failure creeps closer.

A fool with a tool is still a fool.

Implementation of a behavioral focus in an organization occurs any number of ways.

Reward Desired Behavior

In your company, how much is performance evaluated on behavioral measures? How do you reward behavioral alignment? A sales office of a Fortune 500 company was trying to make the transition to a team-based selling approach, and it was working. The systems guys were looking out for the administrative staff, and they were all looking after the salesperson. Sales personnel had such a strong team that the closing rates went up dramatically.

Management rewarded the sales personnel with a high bonus that year. Why not? It was the tool the company had used for years to incent sales performance—but that spelled the end of the teamwork initiative. After the awards ceremony the sales-people were embarrassed and extremely apologetic to the rest of their team: the systems and administrative people. The entire team felt abused by the way the bonuses were handed out. One systems guy had the guts to tell his manager that if they wanted to incent teamwork, they should reward teamwork, not individual performance. Once again a tool got ahead of the behavioral focus. After months of cleaning up the mess, the company now uses team rewards, and everybody's a lot happier.

Too many times, policies and procedures don't align with supporting desired actions and decisions. Here's another example, this one overheard in a conference we were speaking at:

"I want you to fly first class!" a manager chastised an employee.

"Why?" asked the employee, who then defended himself: "I got a much cheaper flight to the same city."

"Because if you don't fly first class, then I have to stop flying first class!" the manager replied.

Apparently this manager was incentivizing the opposite behavior needed to produce a more cost-effective organization.

Behaviorally Select Your Tools

Start evaluating change programs and leadership development from a behavioral assessment, not fashion trends. Before initiating another change program, make sure you're clear on the answers to these questions:

- Will this help us or distract us?
- What impact will this have on the bottom line? Will it further our strategic intent?
- How much behavioral change will be required in our culture?

- It worked in the company referenced in the book, but will it transfer to us?
- What specific behaviors will our people have to do differently for this to be successful?
- Are our people capable of and committed to that behavioral change?
- How much discomfort is everyone willing to endure to make this happen?
- If we're using consultants, will they give us a money-back guarantee if we don't see the results they say we will have?
- What measures will we use to ensure we don't get seduced by this tool and keep focused on the intended result?
- How willing are we to back out if this change doesn't work?

Ignore Résumés

How much of your organization's hiring and selection criteria are behavioral? Résumés are a recollection of what a person did and how he or she did it in the past; it's much like a tool evaluation. But we bet you fire people mainly because of behavioral problems, not a tool problem. So start hiring on behavior. For example, a gate agent at Southwest Airlines told us once, "We can teach anyone to do just about any job in this company other than fly the plane. The problem we're concerned about is attitude. We can't teach that. And that's what we screen for in our hiring process." Similarly, a vet at the Animal Kingdom in Disney World said that even an award-winning vet would not be hired without passing the preemployment test to see if he or she could work well on a team. A brilliant vet who couldn't work with other people would not be hired.

Several approaches are available that bring to light behavioral issues in the hiring process. Options for behavioral interviewing should assess factors such as flexibility, the ability to think quickly under pressure, professional demeanor, ethics, collaboration, teamwork, empathy, respect, and bravery. Companies use a number of methods in this area.

Simulation This school of thought bases itself on simulating an environment or situation to see how the candidate responds, which provides clues on the person's behavioral reactions. Southwest Airlines has job applicants tell a joke to a group—not to see if they're funny, but to see how the audience reacts to them. Given that flight attendants will be spending most of their time in front of a group and trying to have fun, this makes sense. The human resource manager of one of our successful clients, HealthSpring, says, "The interview starts in the waiting room. I have a mirrored window behind which I can see the candidates in the waiting areas. I watch their behavior to see if they are paying attention to or, better still, engaging with the strangers in the room. Given that they will have to engage with our patients, this gives me a clue as to what their future with us could be like."

History Some think that past behavior is a good predictor of future behavior. Perform due diligence on a person's history not by this person, who, after all, wrote the résumé, but by others who worked with him or her in the past. One human resource (HR) manager at an engineering company said, "We ask the candidate if he ever had the challenge of a project being stalled or derailed. Then we ask for people who were involved at the time and interview them to find out how this person behaved in this situation. It gives us a deeper insight into the candidate's natural tendencies."

Behavioral Profiling The technique of behavioral measurement is also useful here. There are hundreds of instruments to determine a person's behavioral profile, including Myers-Briggs. For managers who want to forgo the lengthy training and interpretation required in psychological clinical instruments, faster products like DISC, Caliper, CVI, Profiles XT, and many others are available.[3] These instruments use a questionnaire that typically measures behavior and interprets the person's tendency in such dimensions as dominance/assertiveness, people sensitivity, handling change, attention to detail, problem solving, conflict areas, and team fit. Many group the findings into some sort of four-quadrant profile for ease of assessment.

Most profiling systems have strengths and weaknesses, and some HR professionals say they're all the same, but many show a high statistical accuracy. We recommend using this type of instrument with a combination of other methods. Check with legal counsel on what percentage of hiring decisions can be based on this instrument legally in your state.

Look in the Mirror

In your career, are you too focused on the tools and not the behaviors that are more critical to your future success? Are you trying to use checklists, lingo, and other devices to improve yourself? If so, why not list the behaviors that are critical for your job? Not sure what they are? Ask your manager. Better yet, have your manager list the key behaviors for success in your position, and then evaluate these behaviors as he or she sees them in you. This will give you a clear indication of areas for improvement.

Adapt Your Tools to You, Not Vice Versa

High altitude leadership requires continuous adaptation. Plenty of climbers who died on Everest and K2 have their coveted summit photo frozen in their pockets: all climbers want that shot of themselves at the summit to prove they were there. If they had adapted to the changing environment, they'd still be climbing mountains and snapping pictures for their families and friends.

Similarly, hundreds of dead companies failed to adapt to changing markets, competition, and resource constraints. The next time something goes awry with a new process or change program, face the challenge of recognizing what went wrong with the tool instead of reaching for excuses; accept that you didn't see the impending danger and didn't plan for the unknown, or, gasp, accept that maybe your initial plan was wrong. (The human ego really hates this part.) Recognizing the problem frees you to adapt. Changing your culture to accept adaptation as a way of life drives organizational performance to higher altitudes. Here are a few helpful ideas:

- *Don't overuse policy manuals.* Yes, everyone needs to know the company's holiday schedule, and in these litigious times, you have to add some legal stuff to the manual. But when policies replace thinking or get managers to act from preconceived concepts rather than in a genuine response to fluid circumstances, the company's in big trouble. When it comes to creating rules, use them wisely. After hearing about the Nordstrom employee handbook from someone at a conference years ago, I walked into a Nordstrom office and asked for a copy. What I heard was true. It distilled everything all employees really need to know down to its essence and put it on one card: "Nordstrom Rules: Rule #1: Use your good judgment in all situations. There will be no additional rules." This keeps bureaucracy limited and allows adaptation to changing conditions.

- *Test tool implementations first.* One of the insights from Mike Beer's research in the late 1980s mentioned earlier holds true today: pilot-test any organizational changes before inflicting them on the entire organization. It provides a chance to observe behavioral changes and bottom-line impact and adapt the program before unleashing it on your company.

- *Implement objective danger detection measures.* Adapting tools for changing conditions requires hearing the roar of objective dangers early. When the market shifts and you fail to shift with it or, worse, fail even to notice, you're doomed. The largest wholesale baker in the United States, which developed iconic brands like Hostess Twinkies and Wonder Bread, failed to see the objective danger of the "rising number of old people and sick people and fat people who need less white flour, less sugar, less fat, and more fiber."[4] It filed for bankruptcy in 2004.

- *Start honing the skills to detect and adapt to objective dangers—or letting go of preformed concepts*. Start by assessing your reconnaissance capabilities. The greatest climbers learn how to recognize potential threats like possible avalanche areas, approaching storm systems, or weak snow bridges. But do you have a formal system for your organization to recognize external threats? If so, how good is it at detecting these threats? Call a staff meeting, and review the situation and how to improve it. Consider these ideas:

- Have monthly sales force meetings to present debriefings from the field regarding competitor activity, customer demands, industry changes, and other information.

- Read newspapers. Whether you are a mom-and-pop store or a regional chain, some national player will soon be eyeing the market you created.

- Buy stock in your client companies so you can pay attention to their stockholder reports. Evaluate their financials and strategic plans for the future.

- Buy stock in rival companies. How well are you doing compared to them in such areas as revenue per employee, profit, and top-line growth?

- Invest in an online competitive database service.

- Attend social gatherings or trade association conferences where rival managers may also be in attendance. Flatter them for their superiority. Admire them for their performance. Then listen as they brag about their work.

- Use anthropologists, not market experts, to analyze your market. One CEO approached us after a speech and lamented that a marketing firm's analysis of his clients failed to produce meaningful results. We told him that evaluating current clients can be irrelevant when your success depends on understanding the needs of future customers. He looked shocked when he realized he had wasted his money on an already contaminated target: customers who had already bought into his company, not the new ones he wanted to add.

- Pay attention to the social networking tools like Facebook, LinkedIn, Twitter, or MySpace. (Your teenager will be shocked at how with it you are!) You may find interesting information leaked (on purpose or by accident) by employees or other competitors on new technologies, customer complaints, employee exits, emerging threats, or emerging marketing channels, among others.[5]

- Visit blogs. You will be amazed to see how much information is leaked out in them. These can be blogs written by industry observers, critics, trendsetters, former employees, consultants, and other relevant parties.

- *Readapt plans often.* Once you've identified objective dangers, take action immediately to adapt your plan. You can't afford to wait for next quarter's planning session. Automobile insurance companies were blindsided by Progressive's innovative moves; the major airlines were caught short when Southwest shifted the standards of the industry.

Failure to adapt to changing conditions leads to failure.

Adaptability takes the planning binders off the shelf and makes them living tools. You can have the industry's most efficient system for producing buggy whips, but if everyone is buying cars

Sherpas climbing the ladders in the Khumbu Ice Fall

Chris Warner

instead of horse-drawn carriages, you will go out of business. Just ask the guys still making eight-track tapes.

These survival tips will help insulate you from tool seduction. But don't get too proud of achieving victory, else you get caught by the next danger: arrogance.

Key Learnings

1. Tool seduction sucks profit out of companies.

2. Tools are important, but don't be seduced by them.

3. Detect tool seduction before it consumes the company.

4. Drive from a focus on behavior and adaptation.

5. Adapt your tools to you, not vice versa.

6. Adapt early and often!

The West Face of Ama Dablam (22,349 feet). Chris and his partner climbed directly up this face in the winter.

Chris Warner

Danger #4

ARROGANCE

Don't reach the peak but miss the point.
> —*Dan Jenkins, climber and guide*

Those whom the gods would destroy, they first
make proud.
> —*Sophocles*

Location: Ama Dablam, Nepal

On the most beautiful mountain in Nepal, a vertical spine slices the imposing West Face from bottom to top. To the trained eye of a climber, it is the most dramatic feature on the mountain, but one that remained unclimbed until we showed up.

The mountain is Ama Dablam, and its West Face is legendary. The first team to attempt it, led by Peter Hillary (his father was the first to summit Mount Everest), ended when an avalanche crushed one climber, tearing him from the mountain. When he came tight on the rope, he plucked his partner off the wall. Tumbling, their rope ensnarled a third climber, and all three bodies were caught by Geoff Gabites, whose arm was nearly sliced off by the tightening rope. Legs and ribs were broken. One man was dead. And during the rescue, Hillary's girlfriend was comforted by an Italian climber. That expedition had all the elements of a great novel: an impossible objective, a sordid love affair, a gruesome death, and an act of unbelievable heroism.

These were tough shoes to fill, made more challenging since we were a team of just two, climbing the face in winter.

We spent days in base camp, spying the face with binoculars, trying to understand the patterns of avalanches and rockfall, and tracing the route, like a kid pencils in a maze. We convinced ourselves that the climb would take thirty-six hours, bottom to top.

We were horribly wrong, and our overconfidence almost killed us.

The route proved much more difficult than we imagined. On the second day, we ran out of food. On the third day, we ran out of fuel (so we couldn't melt snow for water). Vertical rock walls demanded that we climb in bare hands, with the temperatures well below zero. My fingers were numb from the second day. We summited at noon on the fourth day. By dinner on the fifth day, we were finally back in base camp.

I crawled into my tent, hoping to peel off a few layers of the stinky clothes I had been wearing for the past five days, but my fingers fumbled with the zippers. There'd been no feeling in them since the second day, but I was too fueled by adrenaline to pay any attention. Now, in the comfort of camp, I realized that nine of my fingers were frostbitten; my flesh had frozen.

Cellular damage from the freezing and lost blood flow makes frostbitten flesh die. Either a doctor has to cut the dead bits off, or they are left to auto-amputate. I whimpered, thinking about losing my fingers. I had plenty of friends with stubs for fingers and feet without toes. It ruined their climbing, and those who lost their noses were pretty hard to look at. Maybe, just maybe, I could save the fingers. No summit was worth this.

Our route directly up that face was described by the media as the most difficult route climbed in the Himalayas that season. It has never been repeated. As for my frostbitten fingers, they never fell off. It took months for the blackened bits to peel away and years for the feeling to return. But today, even a concert pianist would love these long, skinny fingers.

Ever lose nine fingers on your job? A few toes? Your nose? Chris knew body parts fall off when frostbitten, and his blackened fingertips scared some much-needed sense into him. When he and his partner planned the climb, they thought the best way to reach the summit was to break as many rules as they could. As a result, they had:

- So little gear that retreat was almost impossible
- No weather forecasts
- No extra food
- No extra fuel

What they had was dumb luck—and plenty of it. That climb taught Chris the most valuable of lessons: *having too high an opinion of your abilities will kill you.*

We find this insight missing in many organizations, resulting in serious damage to profits and growth. Commonly called *arrogance*, what better laboratory to study its effects on humans than on Everest?

The Everest Laboratory

One of the least hospitable places on earth, Everest's summit holds only one-third the oxygen found at sea level, and the extremely low temperatures generate constant frostbite and hypothermic conditions. Yet even with these conditions, Everest attracts people from all walks of life: hard workers, daydreamers, tick-listers, gracious and humble souls, as well as the most dangerous: those suffering from grand delusions, megalomania, and narcissism. Everest is really no different from any other workplace, except that it is a bit more remote, much colder, and much higher.

After thirty years of failed attempts, Edmund Hillary and Tenzing Norgay finally summited in 1953. Everest became a symbol of conquest for humankind. On its slopes, great acts of heroism unfolded. The mountain turned into an icon, a

Heading for the North Ridge of Mount Everest (29,035 feet)

Chris Warner

compelling saga. At first, Everest was a place where nations demonstrated their national character (whether it be a pioneering spirit or a display of brute power). Then in the late 1970s, it became a place where small teams, seeking adventure on remote faces and ridgelines, defined the Everest spirit. Today, in the age of guided expeditions and televised climbs, reaching the summit of Everest is a deeply personal success.

In the beginning, an ascent of Everest moved humankind a step forward. In the 1960s and 1970s, pioneering new routes on

Everest moved the sport forward. Now tagging Everest's summit moves the summiter forward. No matter your motivation, it is worth the view.

In the best spirit of a compelling saga, people voluntarily put themselves at risk to pursue their dream of standing on Everest's summit. In the fifty-four years since Hillary and Tenzing first summited, more than 4,000 others have followed. With better infrastructure, weather forecasting, and well-staffed commercial operations today, the number of summiters increases annually. No longer just for elite, experienced mountaineers, the mountain has been summited by numerous nonprofessional climbers: car salesmen, teachers, lawyers, and stay-at-home moms—a literal cross section of society. A handful of Japanese men more than seventy years old, three sixteen-year-old Nepali boys and one sixteen-year-old Nepali girl, an eighteen-year-old American girl, a blind climber, and several amputees have summited. In just the spring of 2007, over 540 people reached the top.

But only one thing exceeds the number of Everest's iconic achievements and personal successes: the number of dramatic failures. Between 1922 and 2007, over 13,000 people have tried to climb the mountain. Seventy-three percent of them didn't summit, and 208 of them died. With so much at stake, Everest may be the best laboratory to observe arrogance and how arrogance threatens organizations and profits. And there's no better way to study the practice of leadership in the face of arrogance than as a guide on an Everest expedition.

Location: Mount Everest, Tibet

I first guided Everest, via the Tibetan North Ridge, in 2000. At that time it was more remote and harder than the South Col route, which is accessed via Nepal. The South Col route is the one that Edmund Hillary and Tenzing Norgay climbed in 1953.

In 2000 we were stopped on both our summit bids by gale-force winds. Trapped in a tent at Camp 2, I openly wept when the expedition leader told us to come back to base camp; the trip was over. The client lying in the tent next to me placed his mittens over his eyes and sobbed for an hour. Our dream had ended in failure at 25,000 feet.

It was a bitter failure because we all felt strong, but couldn't catch a break in the weather. We were never given the chance to really test ourselves. And we were deeply disappointed.

Then, on an expedition in 2003, chaos broke loose on the cliffs above the highest camp. I was guiding a team of cameramen, Sherpas, and "contestants" for a reality television show. We were in our tents, resting up for our own summit bid, due to start at midnight. As darkness fell, we discovered that more than forty others were struggling to descend from that day's summit push. They had ignored all the warnings: their slow pace and dwindling oxygen supplies, their freezing toes and fingers, and snow blindness, a condition where the intense sun burns your eyes. In snow blindness, the pain can be overwhelming and your eyes swell shut. Now they were in serious trouble. Instead of resting for own summit bid, a cameraman and I went out into the night, at 27,400 feet, and collected over twenty people. Our team filled our already crammed tents with the worst off, using our oxygen bottles to revive them and burning all of our fuel to make them hot drinks. We spent the night comforting snow-blind, exhausted, and frostbitten climbers. We sacrificed our own summit bid to save those who were so overconfident that they ignored their own inexperience, exhaustion, crowded ridges, and worsening weather and chose to continue anyway.

Their arrogance destroyed our summit bid and put them and us in danger.

In the morning, we began to lower the wounded toward advanced base camp, 7,000 feet below us. I was tied to a man who was snow-blind. A cameraman was helping me guide him. In a steep gully below the camp, we found a Sherpa suffering from altitude-induced cerebral edema (his brain had swelled so much, it was as if someone banged him over the head with a baseball bat). We stopped to fish some medications out of a pack. As I was leaning over, a 6.6-pound cylinder of oxygen was thrown out of a tent by somebody too lazy to carry it down. This cylinder, like a scuba tank with a threaded pipe at one end, sped down a 250-foot snow slope tilted at forty-five degrees. It then launched off a cliff edge and rocketed 85 feet through the air, making direct impact into the back of my skull. The sound was disgusting. I'll never forget it.

I'll also never forget the words that followed. The cameraman grabbed the radio from my shoulder strap and yelled, "Chris is dead! Chris is dead!"

Arrogance places organizations and teams in danger of death every day. Analysts blame organizational failures on strategic missteps, poor market positioning, bad planning, or ineffective execution. But we find that these usual suspects are just the symptoms, not the real cause. The real cause, arrogance, always lurks beneath the surface. Every time a passionate company at the top of its game falls, you find managers who think they already know everything. Ever run into one of them? Managers who think they know everything stop learning and stop questioning, and their arrogance threatens peak performance. Arrogant leaders ignore warnings on mountains and in boardrooms. Their destructive self-absorption as they pursue egocentric dreams is exceeded only by the damage they leave behind by putting others at risk. Sometimes their arrogance infects others, and the incompetent are led to levels beyond their capability. From pure hubris or some hidden fear, arrogant leaders act as if the rules don't apply to them. Because of this, they are frequently outmaneuvered by smaller, more nimble competitors.

**Arrogance occurs when overconfidence infects you.
It chokes the oxygen supply to your brain as
you hallucinate about your own greatness.
Meanwhile, reality slowly fades away.**

How can you tell if your organization has an arrogance infection?

Evidence of an Arrogance Infection

Arrogance is not an acute illness. Its symptoms surface years before the disaster. No one is immune. Lost profits and market penetration happen when arrogance stops leaders from thinking and learning. Over the past century, the words of arrogant leaders gave them away in every industry:[1]

- "Everything that can be invented has been invented."
  —Charles H. Duell, commissioner of the U.S. Office of Patents, 1899
- "This 'telephone' has too many shortcomings to be seriously considered as a means of communication. The device is inherently of no value to us."—Western Union internal memo, 1876
- "I think there is a world market for maybe five computers."
  —Thomas Watson (1874–1956), chairman of IBM, 1943
- "A cookie store is a bad idea. Besides, the market research reports say America likes crispy cookies, not soft and chewy cookies like you make."—Response to Debbi Fields's idea of starting Mrs. Fields's Cookies
- "The concept is interesting and well-formed, but in order to earn better than a 'C,' the idea must be feasible."—A Yale University management professor in response to Fred

Smith's paper proposing reliable overnight delivery service (Smith went on to found Federal Express)

- "We don't like their sound, and guitar music is on the way out."—Decca Recording Co. rejecting the Beatles, 1962

Today, clear and obvious indicators of potential opportunities or threats still continue to go unnoticed by management or ignored until it's too late. This raises the question of accountability. Leaders who avoid accountability for their actions slide down the slippery slope of arrogance quickly, sometimes taking with them as many bodies as possible. Arrogance is what deluded managers at Enron, WorldCom, and Arthur Andersen. They acted as if the rules no longer applied to them. Their employees paid the price for their lack of accountability. And the body count continues to rise. As we write this, Toyota has overtaken General Motors. GM thought Toyota's rise was due to better advertising, not its speed for continuous improvement.

Detecting symptoms of arrogance is harder in companies than on Everest, where you can carry only so much oxygen, and within minutes after it runs out, your fingers and toes grow cold and your problem-solving abilities diminish. (Some of the world's most elite mountaineers can summit Everest without oxygen, but even among the elite, many die trying. Between 1922 and 2006, 759 climbers attempted to summit Everest without supplemental oxygen. Of those, only 144 summited, and 29 died.)[2]

Detect arrogance at lower altitudes by looking around you for the following symptoms. Do employees:

- Stop asking great questions because they think they already know everything?
- Forget who their customers are?
- Already know what the customer wants? Or feel that customers don't really know what they want? Or that management knows better?

- Protect the status quo?
- Ignore or chastise other employees if they propose changes that contradict the expectations of management?
- Seem blind to emerging competition?
- Use aggressive (or passive-aggressive) tactics against each other?
- Spend more time trying to be right versus finding solutions?
- Use meetings to display their "brilliance"?

Still, even when detected, arrogance can persist. A chronic infection, some find it impossible to heal.

Location: Mount Everest, Tibet

I've seen a lot of people die on peaks like Everest. That's why, as a guide, I split the expedition into two teaching segments: the first is where we learn that death is imminent. There are many ways to die on those slopes: getting lost in blinding snowstorms, falling thousands of feet, freezing to death, stroke, or cerebral and pulmonary edema. A broken ankle, an inconvenience at sea level, could spell death on Everest. Run out of oxygen, and your brain stops functioning. Overcome by exhaustion you stop to rest; you'll freeze to death. (At forty below zero, an unconscious person freezes solid in six hours.)

Even though these facts are known by climbers, the arrogant vision of themselves on top of the world, overcoming challenges that stop "normal" people, pulls aspirant summiters up the hill in spite of critical warnings: storm clouds building on the horizon; oxygen reserves being used up; a nagging headache that is actually their brain swelling; exhaustion that makes their movements awkward and their judgments suspect. And these soon lead to blindness, coma, and death. The dramatic tragedies resulting from ignoring such warnings on Everest in 1996 became the basis of the best-selling book *Into Thin Air*.[3]

Instead, they continue upward. Eventually they will stand at the summit, raise their ice ax above their head, have their photo taken, and then turn triumphantly toward home. Most people who die near the summit of Everest die on the descent. The photo of them at the top is still in their camera, buried inside their down jacket, close to their frozen bodies. No one will ever see the photo that captivated their imaginations during the months of preparation, weeks of struggling on the mountain, and hours of extreme effort on summit day.

Death is not uncommon. On the way to the summit, between high camp and the top, you pass over or around seven dead bodies. One is a man with the green boots who lay across the path and died. He is frozen solid. Like a bag of peas left in the back of the freezer, he will never rot. On the way up, he is thankfully on a downward-tilted section of trail, so it is easy to step over him. But returning from the summit, you have to climb up to him and then step over. You are usually forced to stop either just before him or even midstride so you can catch your breath. It is hard for most people to control their breathing when they are straddling a dead guy.

As a guide, I spend a lot of time teaching clients that death will come for them if they arrogantly ignore the warnings. But they rarely heed these lessons.

Similar lessons go unheeded in business as persistent arrogance claims the lives of unsuspecting companies; the process is slower yet no less lethal. You better be watching for it. The price of failure? Death. The onslaught of PC technology against IBM, the steamroller of Wal-Mart over Kmart, and the Southwest erosion of US Air's market share are but a few examples of companies ignoring the clues and the "bodies" because of persistent

Digging out Camp 1 on the North Ridge of Everest

Chris Warner

arrogance. But many of these companies desperately needed the experience. Why? Because they learned the one characteristic that high altitude leaders use to keep arrogance from killing them: humility.

SURVIVAL TIP: Humility

Location: Mount Everest, Tibet

Summit day on Everest can be emotionally confusing and humbling. You are proud to have made it to the final leg of an extraordinary journey, but that pride is quickly tempered by humility as you pass frozen bodies in the course of your journey upward. Like you, these climbers desperately wanted to get that summit photo.

On May 23, 2001, we were all humbled by Everest. Crawling from our tents minutes after midnight, the temperature hovered at minus twenty degrees Fahrenheit. We were swaddled in thick down suits, wearing oxygen masks recycled from Russian MiG fighter jets. In one hand we carried an ice ax; in the other we gripped the ropes.

There were three guides: Andy (the senior guide, climbing Everest for the sixth time), Asmuss, and me (both on our second Everest expedition). We were working with five Sherpas, most of them Everest veterans. The eight of us were leading eight climbers to the top.

Within minutes, Andy started to have problems. He complained that his oxygen mask wasn't working, so I passed him to take over the lead. By 3:00 A.M. Andy had moved to the back of the team. We carried three oxygen bottles apiece, enough for eighteen hours of climbing. At the crest of the North Ridge, we gathered the team and swapped bottles. At this point, one of the climbers, suffering from stomach cramps, descended.

Our team's first climber reached the summit at 8:00 A.M. It was Marco Siffredi, a tremendously strong twenty-two-year-old snow boarder from Chamonix, France. Marco strapped his snowboard on at the top and pushed off. The rest of us, a few hundred feet below, watched as he carved graceful turns down the summit snow pyramid and dropped off a thirty-foot cliff into the Great Coulior, a gully that bisects the North Face. Marco's historical descent, the first ever from Everest's summit to the base, took him less than three hours. My descent stretched on for three days.

At 10:00 A.M., what seemed like the last of the team stood on the summit. Our dream had come true. It was a glorious day. Looking toward the horizon, which must have been a thousand miles away, we could see the curvature of the earth. And next to that arc, the sky was a chalky white color, filled with moisture and dust. Above that layer was a light blue band, then a darker blue bland. And directly overhead, the sky was violet, with stars twinkling in the sky. I remember this vividly, because it was such a surprise. Can you imagine seeing stars at 10:00 A.M.? It dawned on me that I wasn't just on the top of the world; I was standing at the bottom of space. If I could give you a gift, it would be to show you that view. To see those stars, you knew you had traveled to the very edge of our planet.

If your mind was sharp enough, you would also realize something else: you are very, very far from safety. As I realized this, the power of my responsibility crushed down on my shoulders. I was the only guide on the summit. Not far from me were ten members of my team. Andy and Asmuss, along with one other client, were far below, returning to high camp, we hoped. One other client began his descent before dawn so was surely at a lower camp, and Marco was riding untracked powder on his board, earning his rightful place in history.

We took our pictures and started the descent. We had used up nine of our eighteen hours of oxygen to get to the summit. However, that makes it sound too simple. You see, on the way up, we deposited bottles at key stopping points in order to conserve our strength. The one bottle we wore to the summit was now drained of all but two hours' worth of oxygen. The clock was ticking.

Five hundred feet below the summit, we turned a corner of rock and were surprised to see Andy, Asmuss, and one client still ascending the mountain. We descended to them. I explained that they were at least one and a half hours from the summit, perhaps three hours round-trip. They were determined, though, to reach the summit. We conferred by radio with the expedition leader, and they chose to climb up: the summit seemed too close. Andy hoped to tag the top one last time. Asmuss was doing his job, and Jaime, the client, had failed on two previous expeditions. If he were to summit, he would not only be the first Guatemalan climber to reach the summit of Everest. He would also become one of a handful of people to summit the highest point on every continent. The dream of summiting Everest had consumed his whole adult life and had cost him tens of thousands of dollars. If he were to summit now, fame and riches were certain to follow.

At the first oxygen depot, I didn't change my bottle. I knew the three climbers high above me would need it more than I would. I left my bottle next to theirs, knowing full well what this meant: I would run out of oxygen somewhere high on the North Ridge.

It wasn't until my team got to Camp 4 that reports started to pour in about Andy, Asmuss, and Jaime. They had reached the summit, but it had taken them three hours, not one and a half hours. On the very summit, at 2:30 P.M., they ran out of oxygen. Andy unfurled a banner reading, "Abby will you marry me?" Jaime snapped the picture, and they started to descend. At 5:00 P.M. they were spotted through a scope, stumbling toward the spot at which we all had met five and a half hours earlier. Jaime kept sitting down, and Andy was seen lifting him back onto his feet. Jaime was exhausted and was probably starting to suffer from cerebral edema, his gross motor skills already failing.

Asmuss was sent to get the oxygen bottles from the depot. Shouldering over twenty-five pounds worth of oxygen, he climbed back up the slopes. In the fading light, the people manning the scopes could see Andy and Jaime hacking out a shallow shelter and sitting down for the night. They refused to move when Asmuss arrived. We tried in vain to communicate with them by radio. There was no answer.

The history of Everest is full of stories about open bivouacs near the summit. Bivouacking is more miserable than you can ever imagine. In theory, it means sleeping in the open without

a tent for shelter, a sleeping bag for warmth, or a stove to melt
ice to hydrate you. In reality, the chances of survival are limited.
That night, in the very tent of our expedition leader was a
cameraman who had bivouacked near the summit. His partner
died, and he lost the front halves of both his feet.

We pleaded with Andy and Asmuss, if they could hear us,
to please descend. It was better to have one dead person than
three. At advanced base camp, their families were notified
of the situation. Better to let them pray through the night than
to receive one phone call when it is all too late. Abby had
feared such a situation and told Andy that if they were to be
married, he had to give up this lifestyle. Jaime's wife, who lived
in Guatemala and had never seen snow, was oblivious to the
implications. What is a bivouac? "Oh, how nice. Camping under
the stars. Jaime loves stars," she said.

A company driven by a compelling saga still needs a healthy
dose of humility to keep it from veering off into an arrogance
disaster. Humility allows leadership greatness to emerge. Instead
of stepping over weak climbers or leaving them for dead, humble leaders act decisively; the instinct for rescue and recovery,
not refusal and rejection, turns on. When Johnson & Johnson
removed all bottles of Tylenol from the shelves after the poison-
ing sabotage incident in 1982, it did so without hesitation. Its
leadership knew that they had a sacred trust to uphold and that
trust was more valuable than the profits they would lose. They
knew that the rules of human decency applied to them. But too
often we see examples of arrogant business practices enriching
business leaders. As we write this book, it's shocking to hear
about the predatory lending practices that some credit card
companies and mortgage companies have been engaging in. The
results from the arrogance of these managers helped bring
the U.S. economy to its knees.

We are always amazed by the power that arrogance holds over people. When climbers step over others to get to the summit, are they thinking that they have no sacred trust to uphold? Is the world, or even their soul, better off because they summited? We all know businesspeople who say, "It's nothing personal, just business," as they stab someone in the back. In fact, business *is* personal. We spend nearly 50 percent of our waking hours at work each week. How we treat others in the course of conducting our business is the most obvious indicator of what kind of person we are. If you can step over someone in need on the way to the summit of Everest, you will step over people in need wherever you go. If you think that the dying person didn't take that personally all the way to the grave, you've got problems. And some of those problems are going to be tough to explain when it's your turn to be judged in the next life.

Wouldn't your team be better off if people put the team's needs in front of their personal desires? Can you imagine how humbling that would be and how much more satisfying the whole experience would become?

Location: Mount Everest, continued

High on the mountain, the rescue was under way. I worked with an American team that was about to set off for the summit. They carried an extra bottle of oxygen and some medications up toward any survivors. They were to inject the drugs and start the flow of oxygen, while our team of Sherpas raced up the hill with additional bottles of oxygen that were being shuttled from below.

At about 11:30 P.M., Asmuss arrived at high camp. It was the first we were to learn that Andy had stayed behind. A few hours later, the Americans reported finding three Russian climbers huddled behind a rock. They were hypothermic, and some were suffering from cerebral edema.

By dawn the next morning, the Americans found Jaime and Andy. Our Sherpas were not too far behind. And I was organizing high camp into a MASH unit.

Jaime responded well to the steroids and oxygen. Miraculously, he suffered only a tiny bit of frostbite on some fingertips. Andy, however, was in rough shape. Sometime during the night, he had tried to change the batteries in the walkie-talkie. When he took off his mittens, his fingers froze, and he lost the fight to warm them up. Lying in the snow next to Andy were the three parts of the radio and his mittens. He never put the mittens back on. His fingers, nose, and feet were severely frostbitten. The oxygen and steroids revived him, though just barely. The Americans got him to his feet. They knew that his survival depended on giving up their summit bid. Turning around, the small group started back down.

The first Russian to arrive at high camp had tears streaming down his face. One of his partners had collapsed on a ledge and died. Slowly, more people stumbled into high camp. The Russians were guided by a Sherpa working for the Americans. We knew from the radio dispatches that our teammates and the rest of the Americans weren't too far away. Things seemed to be changing from overwhelming to under control: temporarily.

Unfortunately, even after leaders are humbled, they may still have to clean up the mess caused by acts of arrogance. Leadership is a tough job, and no more extreme challenge exists for a leader than to keep leading others through the aftereffects of an arrogance-fueled disaster. Today downsizing, firings, benefit reductions, project shutdowns, budget cutbacks, and other traumas produce an ultimate strain on leadership. There's only one choice: shoulder the load.

A large regional hospital in the United States caught a serious infection of arrogance. The executive team moved out of the main building to a remote country club office where they wouldn't be bothered, and they dressed casually more often than not. They also made fun of the competitor, which was in fact not only doing financially better but excelled at providing service to patients. One of the executives had refused to move and stayed behind because he felt that executives needed to have visibility and credibility with the staff. Ultimately the damage was disastrous. Employee satisfaction dropped to 33 percent, patient satisfaction plummeted to below the tenth percentile, and the hospital was losing money. All the while the executives bragged about how great they were. Arrogance had taken its toll.

A fresh team was brought in to clean up the effects of this disaster. The new CEO fired the remaining executive team who did not leave on their own, except for the executive who had originally stayed behind in the move, and moved all the executive offices back into the hospital. The patient experience, not the country club experience, became the focus. The journey back was tough and long. But after ridding the hospital of the infection, patient satisfaction soared to the sixtieth percentile or higher, employee satisfaction climbed to nearly 80 percent, and financially the hospital is doing better than it ever has. It is now positioned to become the dominant regional player.

Location: Mount Everest, continued

It started as a flash, a sudden movement caught out of the corner of my eye. A climber wearing a bright yellow down suit slid across a patch of ice, went airborne, slammed onto a rock slab, and bounced off the North Face of Everest. I watched as the body cartwheeled through the air, arms spread wide, legs twisting, until it disappeared. Tears poured from my eyes and streamed down my face. I took a deep breath and squeezed the button on the radio, reporting the death to the hundreds of climbers spread among the camps, all listening to our every radio call. At that moment, no one knew who it was. It could have been Jaime, or it could have been any of the Americans. It would be a tortured wait to learn the truth.

I could see more people descending toward the ragged remains of high camp. Most of the tents were stripped, since no one dared to spend another night at this altitude. Normally we would be dead by now, drained by the lack of oxygen. Our time was running out; the adrenaline that kept us going would have to be exhausted. Asmuss was waiting to take Jaime, and I was waiting for Andy. The first American arrived. When asked about the yellow man, he knew all about it. It was the dead Russian, he said, and he pushed him off the trail so no one would have to step over him.

I was shocked. The American thought it was the right thing to do, but watching the brutal slamming of his body into the rock and then bouncing for thousands of feet was heartbreaking. I knew that every time his body slammed into the rocks, more bones were shattered. And if he were ever found, he wouldn't be recognizable. It was a disrespectful way to treat the dead. I later learned that the Russian was named Aleksei Nikiforov. He was the second person to die that day, the third person to die that week, and the fourth person to die that season. He was one of five people to die that year on Everest.

Asmuss took Jaime and lowered him from this camp at 27,400 feet to the camp at 26,000 feet. I took Andy. At 9:00 P.M. we staggered into camp. Andy's frozen fingers, combined with the most profound level of exhaustion, limited his every movement. I unclipped his crampons, unlaced his boots, and slid him into a sleeping bag. His fingers were too numb, so I unzipped his pants and helped him pee in a plastic bottle. I melted some snow, and we drank warm water for dinner.

All night Andy was wracked by rib-cracking coughs. Thick layers of phlegm built up in his throat, and he would hack and hack until they broke free. At dawn, I heard him hacking. Suddenly total silence gripped the tent. At 26,000 feet, a simple breath is so labored that it sounds like you just ran up a hill. The silence startled me. I opened my eyes to see Andy clutching his throat, his lips dark blue, his face turning gray. He was choking to death on his own phlegm.

I unzipped his sleeping bag, unzipped his down suit, then more jackets. I flipped around behind him and, placing my fist tight against his stomach, started to jerk him up and back, up and back. The phlegm popped free, and he sucked in the air. I repositioned his oxygen mask, cranking up the flow, and we sat there, crying and shaking. It didn't seem possible that Andy could survive another hardship, and we were still 5,000 feet above advanced base camp, which was thirteen miles above base camp, which was then eight hours by jeep across the Tibetan plateau to the Nepali border, and another five hours by car to Kathmandu.

Late that night, we finished the descent and limped back to advanced base camp, helped by all our teammates. We would now have to carry Andy the thirteen miles back to base camp. It proved impossible. The ground was all loose rock, boulders, stones, and pebbles, piled on top of a slowly moving glacier. We tried to carry him by stretcher but failed. There was no choice but to strap him to the back of a yak.

If you've ever seen a yak, you can see why they aren't ridden. These prehistoric beasts are mated with cows to domesticate them. Their horns stretch forward, sharpened for protection. Their forward hips are taller than the back ones. Anything that sits atop them is constantly sliding off their rear ends. No culture has built a yak saddle for a reason.

We chose the biggest yak in a herd and pulled it aside. Being a herd animal, it protested as its friends ambled away.

It took us some time to rig a saddle. First, we lay sleeping pads over the animal's back. Andy, in his red down jacket, climbed onto the black beast. It protested under the strain. Andy's feet dangled to the ground, and frostbitten as they were, he wouldn't be able to feel them dragging on the rocks. So with nothing like a stirrup available, we tied a rope to one of his ankles, passed the end under the yak, pulled hard, and tied it to Andy's other foot. He was now strapped onto the yak, but he still kept sliding backward. The yak man grabbed a thin cord and wrapped it around the tip of his finger, thrusting his dirty finger deeply up the yak's now flaring nostril. A finger from his other hand wiggled up the other nostril, fished around for the string, and came out with it. He pulled the string all the way through the yak's nose, like a piece of snot-covered dental floss.

We tied the mucous-covered ends of the string to Andy's hands, and he pulled on these to stay aboard the yak. And with that first pull, a 2,500-pound, barely domesticated animal roared out, kicked violently, and raced away from us, with Andy tied to his back.

It took us thirty minutes to cover the same ground the yak and Andy crossed in minutes. Luckily, the ropes and strings holding Andy atop the yak had not broken. And even luckier, the yak was now out of breath.

Twelve hours after leaving advanced base camp, we arrived at base camp. Twenty-four hours later, we were in Kathmandu. That night as we fell asleep in a bed for the first night in ten weeks, the crown prince of Nepal pulled out a gun and murdered the king and queen and eight other members of the royal family, and then took his own life.

We woke to the wave of panic and protest that gripped the capital. I shoved Andy and our bags in a taxi, and pushing against the crowds marching toward the palace, we arrived at the airport. That day, a half dozen planes landed, a few took off, and then the city was shut off from the world for a week. Andy and I made it out in the nick of time.

I visited Andy a few months later. Parts of his feet and thumbs had been amputated, and he was still recovering from the surgery. I asked him about his summit photos. I needed to see this "Abby will you marry me?" sign.

"Chris, I gave the camera to Jaime. And he ended up snapping a picture of his mitten."

I was deeply humbled by that expedition to Everest. There were too many close calls, the leaders made some poor judgments, and the team depended on luck to keep everyone alive. If the weather had turned for the worse, the three Russian climbers, Andy, and Jaime would have frozen to death high on Everest. A lot of people risked a lot to get those guys down. At the critical moment, when it was time for Andy, Asmuss, and Jaime to turn around, the team felt that the rules didn't apply to them. They continued on to the summit in denial of the obvious risks.

We all learned a lot by guiding Everest. I now tell my clients that even though they paid a lot of money, I don't work for them. I work for their mothers. A client who doesn't reach the summit may be angry with me, but an ecstatic mom welcomes her son or daughter home alive. "I'd much rather deal with an angry client than face the wrath of a mom whose child died on my expedition," I say. When I tell clients this, they get it. They don't like having their moms watching over them again, but on an intellectual level, they know she is the real authority.

I usually don't tell a client that my mom is the person I assume their mom is and that it is her value system that we'll be using to guide our strategy. My mom is an Irish Catholic who works for the church. She believes that we all have a cross to bear and that our daily struggles beneath that cross keep us focused on the only true goal. So I have no problem loading clients up with big packs, and I am not bothered when the expedition turns into an Old Testament–style epic, with blizzards instead of locusts. All those deprivations and trials are good for our soul.

They would be good for any leader's soul. The trial by fire has purged many aware leaders from arrogance. Don's story parallels the mountain narrative:

> I had worked with so many companies that I thought it would be fun and challenging to take over a high-tech company in trouble. I raised capital with some investors because I knew what I was doing, and my confidence (or, rather, my overconfidence) was high. Then the skeletons in the closet came out in full force: employee mutiny against the previous owner, restraining orders, government investigations, technology design flaws, incompetent engineers, and a myriad of other hidden mistakes. Still, I held my head high, arrogantly thinking I had it under control, and I continued the venture capital tour to raise more capital. We needed just another year's runway of cash to fulfill a major order from the largest semiconductor player in the industry.
>
> Then the technology stock market crash came: a trillion dollars lost from the dot-bomb fiasco. It didn't just take the wind out of the sails for early-stage technology investments; it ripped the masts right off the ship! The VC funding dried up overnight. Needless to say, the runway we were funding turned out to be a sheer cliff.
>
> Now I know why some seasoned CEOs I've met said they do deals only with people who've gone bankrupt before. It's the only way to learn. I earned my badge of humility in those days. It's not a badge anyone is proud of, but it is one that leaders desperately need.

How do you bring humility to a team without the "benefits" of a bankruptcy or an oxygen-deprived, freezing environment?

How to Bring Humility to Arrogance

Humility fuels high performance, but is it something that everyone is ready for? No. Not everyone has a strong, confident staff and consistent leadership. Whether on mountains or in companies, we've learned that only solid teams grow stronger when humbled; weak ones become more dysfunctional. Humility causes the weak to question their competence and shatters their confidence. But it shouldn't make you less competent or confident. It should improve your judgment by tempering your ego. As the saying goes, bad experiences teach good judgment, and the better your judgment, the better your performance is.

Crafting an arrogant-free culture takes work, but it's worth the effort. Can you imagine how much more rewarding everyone's day would be if they were surrounded by confident, competent, mature team members who put the needs of the group ahead of their personal desires? If you are a parent, you know how everyone benefits when you put the needs of others before your own. Here are some ideas to make this dream happen in your organization.

Grow Through Failure

Successful people always seek one of the best things climbing teaches you: how to grow through failure. The whole sport is built around pushing limits. You climb until you fall or reach the top. If you aren't falling, you aren't improving. Those pushing the sport forward experience many more failures than successes. These folks don't lack confidence or competence. But they know that the next time they test themselves, they are likely to fail, so they learn to carry themselves with an air of humility.

You must know a few leaders who possess this air of humility. They don't call attention to themselves because they know that their deeds speak for themselves. The same is true of active followers. We all love the people who work hard every single day without feeling the need to call attention to themselves.

Hire Better

Mountaineering provides an easy way to deal with an arrogant climber who may have gotten on the team: unrope the guy at base camp before the mountain does it for you. But in organizations, it means taking more time deciding up front whether an employee should be hired at all. Do your HR people use arrogance indicators in their recruiting and selection process? Do they find out if previous work teams respected this individual, or whether this individual was shot by his or her own troops? Can they admit their own mistakes, or do they always blame someone else? Do they present themselves with an air of humility, or do they seek to impress?

Cultivate Inner Awareness

Achieving humility requires constant work. A momentary lapse in vigilance can result in arrogant behaviors that end up sacrificing the company.

Placing the needs of the group over selfish survival urges is critical in high altitude leadership and requires eternal vigilance.

There was a reason that a Roman slave rode in the chariot with the hero in the parade, whispering to him, "Fame is fleeting." No one is there to whisper to you as you move into the corner office. High altitude leaders require more discipline. Cultivating humility in oneself becomes essential before cultivating it in an organization.

How often do you get feedback from your people on how well you're doing? Or do you care? A recreational sports company was taken over by a venture capitalist who grossly overpaid for the product and in the process inserted himself as president. He decimated the culture of the company so completely that even the investment bankers who took over control were sympathetic to the staff. The president? He denied he had a leadership problem. To this day, he doesn't see how he demoralized, intimidated, and crushed a culture so badly that any possibility of a turnaround evaporated.

Identify and Coach Arrogant Leaders

How can leaders tell if they are infected? Paradoxically, they may never know. Others may be afraid to tell them; staff fear retaliation from the wrath of the boss's arrogance. Listen for what people are saying about the manager. Most times they're discussing the manager's arrogant behavior daily—around the water cooler, while at lunch, or at happy hour. Also listen to the language the manager uses. Is this person always using "I"?

- "Look what I did."
- "Then I took action here and . . ."
- "I thought this would be a good idea and decided to . . ."
- "Of course they were successful. I asked them to do that."
- "When I came here, I . . ."

Handling an arrogant leader is not easy. In one health care firm, the chief financial officer (CFO) was told that his arrogant behavior was frustrating the team. During the performance review with the CEO, the CFO deflected the feedback by attacking the CEO, informing him that the board had been asking about *his* performance. He refused to take responsibility and attempted to bargain or veil a threat—and his days were numbered.

Some executives are enlightened enough to use feedback on their arrogance as a life-changing improvement. Others with a high ego are more pathological and need to be ejected from the organization before they cause too much damage or hurt somebody.

Fire the Weak

Few tasks are more humbling than firing someone. When an arrogant employee isn't coachable, how long do you wait to fire him or her? The short-term pain might be tough to bear, but if you don't fire these people, they will kill your team. A lot of mothers will be angry if your team dies because you didn't have the courage to fire an egomaniac who put personal desires ahead of the group's goals.

Transform Your Meetings

Meetings are great tools—when they work. Typically they don't. At your weekly management meeting, does everyone show up, sit down, and take turns reporting progress on assigned projects? At first glance, this looks like an effective way to ensure accountability for performance, but it could be sabotaging your company's future success. Instead, use the valuable meeting time for what you want more time for: identifying and solving problems.

Problem solving also helps keep arrogance at bay. A good example is a manager at the Toyota Georgetown plant. He used his time in management meetings to demonstrate his good performance on projects until the plant manager, Fujio Cho (who later became the chairman of Toyota worldwide), said to him, "We all know you are a good manager; otherwise we would not have hired you. But please talk to us about your problems so we can all work on them together."[4] This kind of culture keeps arrogance low and the continuing improvement of products high. We mentioned earlier that Toyota has surpassed GM. Could Toyota's meetings be different from GM's? Was Toyota continuously seeking improvements by finding and resolving problems? We bet they were.

This problem-solving versus status-report meeting concept sounds great except for one snag: employees don't like revealing problems. They'd rather reveal their "great performance." Divulging problems could make employees look weak or incompetent or diminish their demonstration of "brilliance" to those who could promote them. More so, it could open them up for retaliation or manipulation. If this resembles your organization's culture, you have work to do.

By maintaining arrogance and not engaging problem-solving behaviors, you miss sharpening your competitive advantage in any market, and profits suffer. Tolerating an arrogant culture guarantees a dramatic financial failure; arrogance has toppled the largest of companies, some of whose executives are now facing prison time. So shift the agenda of your meetings from focusing on performance accolades to sharing and solving problems. Challenge those who say they don't have problems. Are they playing hard enough? Are they holding their cards too close to the vest? Notice the level of defensiveness in the culture. Are people coachable? Can they disclose issues easily? Can they take feedback without it seeming so personal?

Finally, start leading by example: talk about your problems first. This can be difficult, but it shows you are serious, and it allows you to start challenging the group. Start asking questions like these:

- "Even though we are performing well, what's not working or can be improved in your department?"
- "What is your greatest personal challenge or concern we should be talking about today?"
- "Where in your area are you having the most problems?"

This doesn't mean that project performance status shouldn't be on the agenda; a few accolades certainly can be appropriate. But surfacing and focusing on problems and projects that are off course so that the group can work together on resolving them is critical for sustaining competitive advantage and profits.

Key Learnings

- Arrogance infects organizations that aren't eternally vigilant.
- Arrogance sucks profits and destroys even the largest of companies.
- Humility heals arrogance infections.
- Humility shouldn't hinder competence or destroy confidence; rather, it should improve judgment.
- A high altitude leader seeks to learn from failure and continuously improve, and finds arrogance intolerable in a team.

Climbers below the Second Step on the North Ridge of Everest, just past dawn on summit day

Chris Warner

Danger #5

LONE HEROISM

Q: Why do mountain climbers rope themselves
together?
A: To prevent the sensible ones from going home!
—*Anonymous*

Location: Mount Everest, continued

As the descent from the summit of Everest unfolded, I was left shepherding a weakening client and two tired Sherpas. Above us, the last client was still moving upward with the other two guides. Six other clients and three Sherpas were somewhere below us, heading toward the safety of the tents. Every one of us was in a race against time. We started with eighteen hours of oxygen and now had about four hours left. The lower we could get before the oxygen ran out, the greater our chances of survival were.

Remember that above 26,000 feet is the death zone, with less than 35 percent of the oxygen found at sea level, which causes great difficulty in completing simple tasks and problem solving. The results of experiments are shocking: in one experiment, researchers at base camp radioed the climbers, asking some simple math exercises (for example, $12 + 6 = ?$). The oxygen-deprived climbers took minutes, not the usual seconds, to answer. Ask them how much oxygen they have left, and they may not be able to compute the right answer. Ask them to find camp, and they may point in the wrong direction.

Many climbers report memory losses and hallucinations. What seems like a ten-second break to catch your breath is really measured in tens of minutes. The chronic lack of sufficient oxygen leads not only to lapses in judgment, but to frostbite, hypothermia, and high-altitude cerebral (or pulmonary) edema. At high altitude, you can retain so much fluid in your lungs that you drown. The fluid buildup in your brain kills in more creative ways. At first, it limits your fine-motor skills; you can't close a zipper, for example, so you get cold, or maybe you can't clip into the safety ropes. Then it attacks your gross-motor functions, causing you to stumble and maybe fall to your death. As your occipital lobe is compressed, you see wisps of clouds floating inside your eyes, the fog building until you are blind. If you haven't killed yourself yet through some act of negligence, you collapse into a coma. Death follows.

The North Ridge of Mount Everest has three well-known cliff bands bisecting the route, the First, Second, and Third Steps. The First Step is about 150 feet tall and is ascended by pulling on ropes. The Second Step is about as tall but much steeper. This section is so difficult that climbers carried a 30-foot ladder all the way up the mountain and propped it in place. On our way up, we switched from our second to third oxygen bottles on a flat piece of ridgeline, just above the Second Step. On the way down, the Sherpas and clients switched out of their nearly empty third bottle back into the second bottle. These were still 25 percent full, enough to last about ninety minutes. I left my second bottle where it lay so my last teammates, still above, could have it for themselves. That extra ninety minutes might be the very difference they needed to get down at their slow pace.

Lying facedown in the snow and gravel, just above the Second Step, was a famous Spanish climber. He had climbed to the summit of Everest without bottled oxygen, and now that tactical decision was killing him. His Sherpa stood above him, tears in his eyes. The Spaniard had gone blind.

I rolled him over and listened to his moaning. He needed two things: oxygen and a dose of the steroids that reduce this type of swelling. I knew that with help, he could swallow a dexamethasone tablet and wash it down with a sip of water. If this treatment didn't work, I would then pop a stronger, injectable dose into his butt.

He greedily ate the dexamethasone and let us help him stand up, but he wouldn't let himself use any of our oxygen. He was filming his ascent for Spanish TV and desperately wanted this to be an "oxygenless" ascent. Purists look down on climbers who use oxygen when climbing, and on the Spaniard's first ascent of Everest, he had used it. Now he wanted a "pure" ascent to prove he was among the sport's elite. (In contrast, it has long been considered irresponsible for guides to lead clients to the summit without using supplemental oxygen.)

Lone heroism is dangerous. We're not talking about the lone challenge we sometimes take on for our own personal development (just like Chris's lone attempt on Shisha Pangma, which we'll get to later), but the ego-driven, selfish, glory-seeking heroism. We see this in aspirant leaders as they use others to get where they want to go, stepping all over people without even removing their crampons. Is this happening in your organization? Is it happening to you?

Who is keeping programs and projects "pure" in your company? Who is trying to do it all, alone, without supplemental support? Who thinks it's a sign of weakness to ask for help? Or, worse, who thinks he or she is the lone hero—the only one who can do something right? You know the mantra: "If you want something done right, you have to do it yourself."

Lone heroes didn't create the problem all by themselves. We've all admired the lone hero, even made movies about them. We've worshipped this type of leadership to a fault. But imagine how much more productive companies would be if lone heroes spent less time proving their superiority and more time producing results. The former saps organizations of their vitality. Similarly, the Spaniard's narcissism may just kill him.

Location: Mount Everest, continued

It took all of us a precious half hour to lower the Spaniard down the hundred-foot cliff. I was standing on a ledge little wider than a phone book, clipped into the fixed ropes, waiting for him and my last client and the Sherpas. Landing next to me, the Spaniard refused to clip into the ropes. He had convinced himself that any help from us would negate the purity of his achievement. Now he was outwardly angry and pushed past me. He wanted to get off the mountain as fast as he could and wouldn't be bothered by safety practices, like attaching himself to the ropes. There was nothing I could do to stop him. If we even bumped into each other, he'd fall off the mountain. And I couldn't follow him, to talk sense into him, without abandoning my own teammates.

His Sherpa was the next to arrive on that tiny ledge. He had a radio, tuned to the expedition's frequency. I held it in my hands, pushed the button, and broadcast to anyone who might be listening that their climber, the most famous mountaineer in Spain, had been found, blinded by cerebral edema, above the Second Step. They needed to know that we were trying to rescue him and that he was uncontrollable. They did have one other Sherpa in high camp and dispatched him to help us, but help was still hours away.

At the top of the First Step, two Austrians grabbed the Spaniard. He was about to run off the sloping dome, which starts at a gentle angle and then turns into a hundred-foot-tall cliff. They held him until I arrived. The Spaniard, insisting he was fine, clipped into an old rope and started to lower himself off the cliff's edge. He mistakenly chose the oldest rope of the bunch, one that stretched only halfway down the cliff. As if he was fated to live, the very end of that tattered rope was tied with a bunch of messy knots that stopped him from sliding off the end and free-falling down the North Face to his death.

I grabbed a second rope and rappeled down to him, transferred him onto my rope, and waited at the bottom for him. I waited, with one of the Austrians, on a crowded ledge no bigger than a dining room table and tilted just steep enough for most things to spill off. We stood next to Fran, who was dressed in a faded purple down jacket. She had been lying there for exactly three years.

Although not a lone hero herself, Fran's story shows how unforgiving Everest can be to victims of the dangers of selfishness, tool seduction, and arrogance. Fran was an American mountaineer, climbing with her Russian husband as part of a larger expedition. The couple was also climbing "pure," without oxygen. They reached the summit at 6:15 P.M. on May 22, 1998.

Fran and her husband realized far too late that they had overestimated their capabilities; both were too exhausted and weak to make it back to high camp. They spent the night high on the mountain, huddling together on a tiny ledge, with no tent for shelter or sleeping bags for warmth. The next morning, they mistakenly separated on the descent. A few hours later, a team of five climbers passed the husband and later came upon Fran. They made some attempts to get her moving, giving her both oxygen and medications. But in the end, the lure of the summit proved too strong for the potential rescuers, and Fran was left to descend on her own.

During the six or eight hours she was alone, she didn't move too far. The five summiters spent some time with her on their descent. They lowered her off the First Step and attached her to an anchor. They also gave her some oxygen and then continued their return to high camp. Meanwhile her husband made it back to the highest camp, at 27,400 feet. Knowing that Fran needed him, he crawled from the tent and set off to save her—alone, without help. He carried a thermos of tea and a bottle of oxygen.

The last of the five summiters passed him at 8:40 P.M. When he finally found Fran, she was alive, but even with his help, she couldn't move. We can speculate that he left her to go back to camp for help, finally realizing he could not do the job alone. His body has never been found.

At dawn the following day, a South African couple climbing with four Sherpas and a team of three Uzbekhi climbers came upon Fran. She was still alive, having somehow now survived two nights out in the open. They tried to give her some help, but must have felt it was in vain. Tears in their eyes, the South Africans and one Sherpa turned back, while three Sherpas and the three Uzbekhis went to the summit. Fran died late that afternoon.

Location: Mount Everest, continued

So here we were, on one of the most tragic ledges on all of Everest, trying to help a man who was so whacked out from chronic oxygen deprivation that he fought all of our efforts to keep him alive.

The Austrian and I yelled and screamed at the Spaniard as he stopped mid-cliff and for some reason disconnected from the rope. Was he planning to jump to his death? He eventually down-climbed a bit, then jumped. The Austrian actually tried to catch him. It seemed suicidal to me. They could have both tumbled to their deaths. By a miracle, the Spaniard landed safely next to us.

My own client and the Sherpas were still descending the First Step. I needed to wait for them. Luckily for us all, some divine being was keeping the Spaniard alive. On these less steep slopes, he would race ahead of us, then stop and wait. At one point, he jumped down a small cliff and thought he broke his leg. He looked at me with tears in his eyes, "Can you help me with my broken legs?" "Get up!" I demanded, my anger getting the best of me. He forgot his legs were broken, now more fearful of me. He pushed, I pulled, and he stood. "I guess they are not broken," he said, and with that, he scrambled on. It was the last I saw of him, but not the last I heard from him.

Later that night, the Spaniard was found outside some tents at 26,000 feet. The climbers who found him dragged him into their tent. Because of this act of kindness, they were now giving up their summit bid to save him.

There's another problem with lone heroes: they're never grateful for the help they're given. Did the Spaniard appreciate the great sacrifices made by strangers, who were risking their own lives and giving up their own summit bids, to prevent him from becoming just another frozen monument on Everest? No. In fact, he was really angry at everyone who tarnished his lone hero image. We didn't exactly get a thank-you card from the Spaniard.

Location: Mount Everest, continued

The Spaniard returned home, learning that some of his countrymen had publicized his "rescue." It was a major blow to his ego, especially after he had fought so hard to summit Everest without oxygen. I was the first person he attacked in the climbing press. He denied everything. He was certain he was never helped, certainly not by an American. I received vicious e-mails from his fans. One e-mail said among many things that I was the biggest *&$%^# in mountaineering.

The Spaniard eventually wrote a book about his historic climb. I haven't read it, but can only guess that it treats those of us who worked so hard to get him down as another nuisance he had to overcome. A few years later, the same Spaniard was rescued on K2. Again he was climbing without oxygen, starring in a televised program. His team summited late in the day. He became lost on the descent, was found semiconscious by a teammate, and was dragged to camp. He suffered severe frostbite, losing all his toes.

A few years after that, an Irish climber collapsed on the North Ridge of Everest. Over forty climbers are said to have passed him in the hours before he died. Many spoke with him, but no one made any rescue attempt. When the famed Spaniard was asked about this incident, he replied, "It's a classic [on Everest]—someone is in trouble, and people pass by, not even taking a quick look at him."[1]

Lone heroes make for great cinema, but in death zone environments, they become frozen corpses. Unfortunately, in today's companies, many strive to pursue the hero's drama: to be the one who saves the day, the lone hero whom all will admire. You see it every time a manager gets sucked into operations to compensate for the weak teams or poor accountability they themselves created. Or you hear it in the bragging and swaggering at meetings when someone name-drops or tries to highlight his own brilliance.

Lone heroes are often tolerated, ignored, or backstabbed in after-hours meetings. For high altitude leaders, however, the damage from lone heroes is unacceptable.

How Lone Heroes Endanger Organizations

Lone hero damage can be found in every organization. In extreme cases, military organizations know this all too well. Don's father was a POW. Don interviewed POWs from the Korean War who showed up at his dad's funeral; they would talk to him openly now that his father was dead. Before then, it was not honorable to speak openly; it was part of their code. Among the many stories he heard were those about the damage from self-styled "heroes" who would challenge their captors. Watching too many John Wayne movies made these guys opportunists, demonstrating their manhood by challenging the guards. In the end, these lone heroes ended up angering their captors, who then took their frustrations out on the whole group.

Other stories told by Vietnam veterans tell us that it was these same lone hero types who would put their own troops at risk. These heroes wanted to look good to the upper brass, get their ribbons, and climb higher in the military organization. Not surprisingly, many ended up getting fragged by their own men. (Fragging occurs when a soldier kills a superior officer or a non-commissioned officer. It originated from the use of a fragmentation grenade in the murder.) "During the years of 1969 down to 1973, we have the rise of fragging—that is, shooting or hand-grenading your NCO or your officer who orders you out into the field," says historian Terry Anderson of Texas A&M University. "The U.S. Army itself does not know exactly how many . . . officers were murdered. But they know at least 600 were murdered, and then they have another 1,400 that died mysteriously.

Consequently by early 1970, the army [was] at war not with the enemy but with itself."[2] Apparently soldiers will die for their country, but not for a lone hero's selfish career advancement.

Today the Defense Department wisely trains U.S. troops in a concept they call "no heroes," which means working as a team, an integrated system. Don witnessed a demonstration of this when on tour as a guest of the secretary of defense. After seeing troops in an "asymmetric attack protocol," a demonstration of comprehensive coordination and teamwork, he remarked that he was glad he wasn't on the opposite side. This "no heroes" concept has tremendous value in the boardroom as well.

Does your organization have leaders who sabotage others or work groups suffering from lone hero mistakes? If so, the damage can be extensive. We find these negative impacts on a company from lone heroism:

- *Weak teams.* A weak management team full of lone heroes handicaps performance tremendously. Not only are they unable to contribute meaningfully, they thwart critical decisions and actions necessary for achieving vital goals.

- *Low accountability.* Lone heroes may not have a team around them to hold them accountable or, worse, they may usurp accountability from others by taking on other people's jobs. Then, in an accountability vacuum, everyone wonders why nothing is getting done.

- *Misaligned direction.* Whether they are conscious of it, lone heroes putting their personal agendas ahead of the organization's goals, misdirect resources and slow people down.

- *Demoralization.* No one wants to work with someone just to make that person look great or become rich. Will your team have to frag the lone hero to save themselves?

- *Hostages.* Often managers are too afraid to fire a lone hero because they begin to think these people really are heroes. They are led to believe they can't do without this employee.

Lone heroism can be found contributing to higher operating costs, lower innovation, increased risks, delayed execution, higher turnover, and missed sales opportunities. But lone heroism is not a natural phenomenon. There were no successful John Waynes in human evolution. Archaeological evidence points to communities of tribes having higher survival rates than lone individuals. In fact, banishment from the group emerged early in history as a serious form of punishment. The lone hero's journey makes for compelling literature, but in real-life human experience dating back to the earliest prehistoric times, it typically equates with failure and death.

When studying lone heroism we found that high altitude leaders choose a different path: partnership.

SURVIVAL TIP: Partnership

Location: Broad Peak, Pakistan—Second Attempt of the World's Twelfth-Highest Mountain

The sun was dipping on the horizon. At 26,000 feet, we were just 400 feet, but still two hours, from the summit. It was too late to continue climbing, but we didn't want to give up. If we could bivouac where we were, we should be able to reach the summit in the morning. It was time to dig a shelter into the nearest snowbank. If we could find the perfect spot, we could build a snow cave, protected from the wind, in which to hide out for the night. Of course, the lack of a sleeping bag, sleeping pads, and the other luxuries was just an inconvenience. With a good shelter, we would survive a night and, we hoped, be frostbite-free in the morning.

I rounded a hump on the ridge and saw that two Poles also had the same idea. All the other teams had already turned back.

The Poles were scooping out a sad-looking hollow in the snow. I thought I spotted a better place. I dug and dug, good snow cave engineering tips colliding in my brain. Beneath a layer of wind-crusted snow lay a pocket of sugarlike snow, all finely grained and not sticking together. But even with my partner sliding face-first into the hole, we couldn't seem to make the space big enough.

As the sun set, our cave was barely long enough and too tight, so we kept digging. Finally, when we both tried to lie down in it, my breathing went haywire. Something about spending the night crammed into a double-wide coffin at 26,000 feet, with no room to wiggle and the icy top just inches from my face, while super-cooled, oxygen-depleted air poured over me from a manhole-sized exit slightly above me, through which blowing snow could cover my face and slowly but surely suffocate me, made me a bit overanxious. The sun set. I still couldn't control my breathing. I was having a silly little anxiety attack just because my bed wasn't ideal. Pitiful.

I climbed out of the hole. I didn't care how cold and miserable the Poles looked in their hovel; I was prepared to join them. "No problem," they said. "We are going down in fifteen minutes." No explanation was possible in the blowing wind. The night was surreal enough. As I stood outside the two caves, the moon already high in the sky and the sun long since lost below the horizon, I heard distant shouts. It sounded as if the descending climbers were moving slowly. I had no idea that another Pole had broken his ankle (or lower leg) and that a rescue was unfolding.

The two Poles popped out of their scoop in the snow, grunted their good-byes, and headed into the darkness. My partner and I moved into their roomier but airier hole. The wind blew snow on top of us. We strategized our survival plan.

Three things are critical to surviving in those conditions: insulation, discipline, and a willingness to cuddle with anyone.

Insulation: We had only our down jackets and pants, our mittens, and our packs. We laid our packs on the ground and used them as tiny mattresses, hoping to insulate our vital organs from the ice-cold ground.

Discipline: We had a stove and pot with us. It became critical to drink warm liquid every few hours. It was also critical that we keep track of every piece of gear and clothing and that we never allow ourselves to drift into hypothermia.

Cuddling: Our only source of heat was each other, and our most vital body parts were our feet. If we left our feet inside our boots, both of us would suffer frostbite and possibly be unable to walk in the morning. We took off our boots and started to rub our feet. Then when we were ready to settle in for a few hours of escapism (I slept like a baby while my partner fiddled and fidgeted), we needed to put each other's feet inside the other's jacket for warmth.

Try this at home. Lie down with your partner in one of those top-loading freezers. Each of you should be on your side. Then entangle your legs over and around each other, slipping your feet deep into the other's jacket. When your partner whines loud enough, start to rub his toes. Get the blood to flow into the heels. And just when the pain in your hips gets too great, you both must unknot, roll over, and tangle up again. While this is happening, your feet start to refreeze.

Every few hours, we disentangled to heat some water. High above, the moon bathed the world in false daylight, with all the brightness but none of the heat. We figured the sun would hit us at 6:00 A.M., but it seemed to get snagged on a rock outcrop not fifty feet away. We continued to cuddle.

The wind grew stronger as the sun rose, and loose snow started to fill our hole. Slowly we stood up and saw plumes of blowing snow whipping from the summit like a giant white flag. Our boots were frozen solid and nearly impossible to put on. Our hands froze and refroze as we tugged on the laces and tied sloppy knots.

The sun was still stuck on the rock above us. The waving white flag of blowing snow tearing from the summit made the choice obvious. We could see the true summit. It seemed so close. But the ferocity of the winds reinforced the message. Before we could strap on our crampons, the winds and growing humidity combined to cap the summit with a lenticular cloud—the cloud most feared by all climbers because it signals high winds (think of them as stationary hurricanes guarding the summit).

We were sad, yet relieved, to beat a retreat from our little hole in the snow at 26,000 feet. We dropped down to a steep-sided but well-marked trail carved in the snow. A few hundred feet lower, we saw some abandoned ice axes and ski poles, and below them a telltale track in the snow where someone had tripped and slid a short way.

At an awkward crevasse, we met an Iranian climbing upward. His English was worse than my Farsi, but I think the look on our faces, combined with the now storm-force winds above, should have convinced him to turn back. He climbed on.

Later we came across an Italian. He was still in sight of Camp 3, but he was heading up. He spoke little English, asked for water (which we had none), and climbed into the storm.

At Camp 3, a frantic Italian grilled us about their missing friend. It was the same fellow we had passed an hour ago. He had been on yesterday's summit bid. He had fallen asleep on the descent and in the dark slept unnoticed by all the other descending climbers. Delirious, he was now reclimbing the mountain. No one seemed to know anything about the Iranian. (Both climbers later made it down okay.)

Just above Camp 2, we met two Americans. They were glad to see us, but were busy laying rope for the rescue of the Pole with a broken ankle.

There is a twist to the story of the injured Pole. A few days earlier at Camp 2, we had gotten into a conversation. "Artur,"

I had asked him, "you climbed four of the world's tallest peaks, many by new routes or in winter. Why have you returned to climbing after a retirement of fifteen years?" Artur explained, "My wife, she comes down to the kitchen table and says, 'Artur, you are getting old and fat. Go back to the mountains and come home a skinny boy.'"

We climbers never seem to win.

High altitude leaders know that partnership with peers, staff, or outside stakeholders trumps lone heroism every time. You might think that if there's a fire, you have to be the one to grab the fire hose and put it out. But the hard, tough question is, "How come you're alone?" Is the team under you so weak that it can't handle the problem without your heroic rescue? Or are you alienated from your peers? Isn't there a partner willing to help? How's that lone hero act working out for you?

Partnerships are different from teams. Sometimes you partner with people who aren't on your team, or even in your organization. Other times teams need a partner to help them work. Or you may partner with just one person, not a group. Sometimes teams can exhibit partnership, but many are just committees or work groups where the relationships are perfunctory or transactional.

Contrast the above story with the division president of a private power plant company. His only agenda seemed to be to look good to the boss and be seen as the lone hero. He truly felt that he was the source of the company's success and set his sights on taking over the holding company that owned the utility. Unable to conceive that he needed support from employees and his peers, he alienated himself and was eventually sabotaged in his projects and initiatives by other employees—a business-world version of fragging—and ended up leaving the company.

**Earth Treks teams passing below the summit
of Mount Cotopaxi (19,348 feet)**

Chris Warner

How to Bring Partnership Forward

Creating partnerships in your life raises different questions. How many projects are you leading alone? Where are you resisting support from others? Who can you bring in to help you or your team summit bigger peaks? As you seek to bring partnership forward, remember:

- You don't need an equal or superior to create great partnership. Genuine partnership is never truly among equals. Leaders are not all created equal. Partners can come from all levels.

- Pass the mantle of leadership to whomever is equipped to take it in the moment. In the face of life-threatening circumstances, who can afford to be hesitant? The same applies to critical business functions or even your own career development.

- If you're the team leader or manager, sometimes you have to get out of the way. How does a boss give up running the show to someone else without abdicating his or her role? In true partnering, one "gives up" control by empowering key talent and letting accountability drive the results.

- Partnerships don't work well with leaders who are so afraid of losing control that they end up allowing only weaker people to work under them.

- Create and maintain vibrant partnerships by maintaining accountability. If you've embraced death, crafted a compelling saga, focused on behavior, and mastered humility, then you are ready to allow partnership to drive peak performance.

In the early 1990s, Don was on a team that worked with DuPont when it faced a crushing combination of challenges: increasing environmental regulation, the ever-more-complex logistics of globalization, and an intense pressure to control spiraling costs. The Information Technology Department in the company's Chemical Division reorganized and responded faster than all the other divisions because its teams rotated leadership based on the situation, while at the same time consistently supporting each other in meeting accountability requirements. The approach was so effective that one of the departments received the Team of the Year Award from the American Association of Training and Development.

Here are some implementation ideas for partnership development:

- Create a professional mastery group. Partner with others in your professional area to support each other in learning and applying best practices and other dimensions useful for peak performance. These could be groups focused on particular areas such as sales, manufacturing, quality, customer service, or finance. The concept, similar to the original professional guilds, can be applied anywhere. Many industry associations can help here.

- Create a career development team. Partner with peers to give you feedback, ideas, and accountability support to keep you focused and on track in your career growth. The focus is on business and professional life. Team members can be career-focused peers both inside and outside your organization. Let them help you gain skills, career speed, and confidence.

- Find a stalled or derailed project you are responsible for. Which partners could help get it back on line? Call them!

- If you're running a company, join a CEO group to help you survive the dangers; challenge your selfishness, arrogance, and tool seduction; and make you feel comfortable with being uncomfortable. Two groups we mention in the Acknowledgments, Vistage and YPO, hire Don frequently to speak to their groups. Don himself is a Vistage member.

Key Learnings

- Lone heroism sucks profits because of the resources necessary to contain or clean up the damage it causes.
- Lone heroism demoralizes others.
- Lone heroism can lead to manager fragging.
- Partnership drives peak performance by engaging and leveraging the team's strengths.
- Partnerships use accountability and a compelling saga to drive performance.
- There are no more messianic leaders. The few who came before aren't interested in working for your corporation. You'll have to settle for creating powerful partnerships.

Chris Warner on Broad Peak, with K2 in the background

Tao Franken

Danger #6

COWARDICE

I think risk is important. I don't care if it's a great
financial risk or a physical risk.

You only get out of something what you put into it
and the fact that you are willing to risk something
means that you are going to get a lot more out of it.
—*Yvon Chouinard, climber, surfer, and founder*
of Patagonia, the clothing company

Location: Broad Peak, Pakistan: First Attempt

All the good weather came in June while we trekked to base
camp and set up lower camps. Once we were ready to make some
real summit bids, the deep snow and bad weather conspired
against us. In early July, most of the team collected at Camp 2 on
Broad Peak, despite our normal pattern of each person doing
whatever he or she pleased. I had been working on Broad Peak
for the first few weeks, figuring that it was safer to acclimatize
here than on the more dangerous K2. Every time I tried to make
a summit bid, I was pushed back. Two of us made one fast and
superlight bid, but deep snow slowed us to a futile crawl. On a
later solo attempt, the wind tossed my tent up and down while
I huddled inside, fully dressed, my pack on my back, waiting for
the storm to either blow itself out or tear the tent apart. The
storm had come from nowhere and with tremendous force. At
dawn, I collapsed the tent and retreated to base camp. On my
last try, I wasn't alone on the peak. A thousand feet above us,

a team of Japanese and Koreans was camped. And a thousand feet above them, two of our teammates were camped. In the tents surrounding me were just about everyone else from base camp. We all smelled the summit.

We were climbing from Camp 2, at 21,000 feet. The summit was almost 5,500 feet higher, which meant it would be a long summit day. At 9:00 P.M. we all left camp, the lights of my teammates quickly disappearing as they raced out of camp. I paced myself. About an hour into the climb, the first two climbers dropped out. Three hours into the climb, I passed three more as they huddled in the remains of an old Swiss tent. A bit above this, I caught up to three more. Above us, we could see the lights of the Koreans and our two friends. Passing their tent at 23,500 feet, a tired Italian on our team decided to quit and crawled into one of the Koreans' tents. The remaining three of us soon caught up to our two friends, then to the Koreans. The folks out front were severely slowed by the deep snow. At 3:00 A.M., we reached the final slopes up to the col, the saddle that separates the central and main summits.

The snow, which had been knee-deep, now reached to our hips. And the path we were creating, a once-rising traverse, turned straight uphill. Directly in front of us, a crevasse bisected the logical route to the top. We pulled out a rope, and I set off, crossing a snow bridge and then attacking the steep but bottomless snow slope. One slip and I would bounce into the crevasse. But the greater danger was triggering an avalanche. With that much snow lying on that slope, it seemed suicidal to continue. So I prodded some more, hoping that my partner would hold the rope if I suddenly was swept away by an avalanche. But in that deep, soft snow, I couldn't get an anchor to hold. I tried placing them, but every little tug that my partner gave, the anchor popped loose, like toast. There was no way to safeguard against the obvious dangers.

I gave up and with me went my two teammates. The Koreans gave it a go, spending another hour shoveling snow, but getting no more than a dozen feet higher. We met our two friends on the descent. Our Italian teammate who had quit earlier heard us returning and crawled from the tent he borrowed to get the latest news. We told him all about the snow, at 25,500 feet: it was too deep and soft and likely to avalanche. We were stopped about 200 vertical feet from the col, from where the rocky ridge to the summit, especially at this early hour, would never be able to stop us.

Back at base camp, the Italian wrote authoritatively about the climb, the snow conditions, and the decision to turn around, sharing it with all the Web sites. However, he omitted the part about his quitting and crawling into someone else's tent for a nap.

This wasn't my first experience of hyperbole being used by the world's "best" mountaineers. After a few seasons on Everest, I had come to expect this kind of stuff, but by the commercial operators playing a marketing game, not by real climbers just playing on a peak most considered easy. I was soon to learn that the so-called best would rather the world didn't know the truth.

Cowardice endangers organizations just as badly as its opposite cousin, lone heroism. Did you ever have someone in your company boast about her heroic efforts when in reality he or she wasn't even close to the action? Maybe the Italian knew some things the others didn't (or maybe he just couldn't keep up). But it reminds us of the oft-repeated movie scene where the pompous politician, faced with risk, hides until the fight is over, only to emerge later as if he had been a significant part of the action. Unfortunately, such behavior infects all kinds of teams and cultures, in mountaineering and elsewhere.

At The SAGA Leadership Institute, whether we're teaching executive workshops, speaking at conferences, or facilitating off-site corporate retreats, one common theme emerges from the participants: they want to know whether they are getting straight answers from staff. Managers feel frustrated when they discover something wrong when it's too late to fix it, realize that a project was doomed from the start, or hear uncomfortable feedback about them that they should have had earlier. Why is it that many people never speak up? What holds them back? The progeny of all previous dangers: cowardice.

Is your company infected by cowardice? Do doomed projects move ahead because the cowardly don't dare reveal the truth? Do staff members talk behind their manager's back because their cowardice prevents them from confronting the obvious? Has cowardly politics overtaken performance? If so, you can bet some employees prefer crawling into a tent for safety rather than risking their necks by exposing the truth or challenging the status quo.

Risk avoidance risks companies.

How Cowardice Risks Companies

Fear of failure, or fear of consequences like retaliation, being ostracized, being blamed, or looking bad to the boss, propels cowards into the tent of safety. But not high altitude leaders. These leaders push the limits of performance and don't allow the friction of cowardice to jeopardize the future. In a world where innovation, competitive superiority, and market growth are fraught with risk, cowardice is a danger few companies can afford.

Cowardice damages companies by stopping people from exhibiting high altitude performance behaviors like these:

- Challenging others on their lack of accountability
- Exposing weak members of a team
- Confronting arrogance
- Uncovering selfishness

- Acting during a time of real need even when it requires personal sacrifice
- Divulging the state of doomed projects
- Admitting our own faults
- Challenging lone heroes
- Developing partnerships
- Pushing people past their comfort zones
- Eliminating the seduction of the latest management theory
- Challenging others to say the unsaid
- Making brave decisions

We're sure you can extend this list indefinitely. Cowardice is clearly a big problem. Like many of the other dangers you've learned about, cowardice also is biological. Anthropological studies of both ancient and contemporary cultures reveal intriguing insights into the nature of cowardice within groups. But after thousands of years, what is the best practice for dealing with cowardice? Consistently, high altitude leaders throughout history found a way: inspire bravery.

SURVIVAL TIP: Bravery

High altitude leaders recognize the value of bravery and become frustrated when training and organizational development programs rarely inspire it. Few even know how to train for it. Because of this, businesses typically suffer losses of innovation and improvement, and strategic execution suffers—all manifestations of the absence of courage in the workplace.

Cowardice can only be dealt with head-on, by creating a context in which people's unstated agendas and whispered concerns are given voice—a context in which genuine risk taking is not only encouraged but insisted on. We're not talking about recklessly pursuing stupid risks, but instead generating a

Walking over a ladder that spans a crevasse on Everest

Chris Warner

courageous culture—one where employees speak the truth and expose the real issues about failing projects, political infighting, weak management, and unpopular but real market shifts.

Is your organization ready for bravery? What if you delay confronting this danger for just another few years?

How to Instill Bravery

High altitude leaders instill bravery by turning cowardice into bold action and profitable growth. The methods they use can be controversial and are often not taught in business schools. Only a few dare venture into this harsh environment that requires politically incorrect techniques. The one used by many ancient civilizations is a good first step: shame.

Shame

Yes, shame induces bravery effectively. The approach varied among cultures, but the techniques were fairly simple:

Cowards go into battle, even though they're scared to death, because they're too ashamed to turn and run in front of their peers.

After a few battles, cowards find their own legs, and there's no discernable difference between the born brave and the learned brave. Thus, shame induces bravery. Anthropological studies find the methodical application of shame for the eradication of cowardice common among many cultures—except modern corporations.

Shame is no longer politically correct. The pendulum has swung from using it to change behavior to seeing it as the destroyer of fragile self-esteem. Today's leaders, consultants, and trainers find it easier to ignore past conflicts, pains, and disasters than to confront theses issues. They promote the theory of creating a "desired future" and focusing on building self-esteem instead of dragging up the past. But this theory fails in practice. Building self-esteem may seem to be a noble and wonderful idea, but exhaustive research tells us that self-esteem has little to do with achieving success.

Courage is the first of human qualities, because it is the quality which guarantees all others.

Winston Churchill

Roy Baumeister, a professor of psychology, along with a team of researchers, reviewed thousands of studies of self-esteem. With all the talk about its importance, the societal changes we've made to boost it, and so forth, you would think that they found proof positive of its impact on academic and workplace performance. But Baumeister has observed, "There is not nearly as much benefit as we hoped. It's been one of the biggest disappointments of my career."[1]

Feeling good about yourself, having fun, or thinking positive thoughts is nice, but that isn't what gets the job done. In fact, a team culture that focuses too much on praise and too little on criticism might breed a team full of narcissists.

Fun is a by-product, not a goal.

We saw this in a health care client that had been struggling with low employee satisfaction scores for years. By using a "shameful" approach to disclose unpleasant truths about who wasn't fulfilling leadership potential, it painfully raised the issues so necessary for performance. The result? We helped them drive employee satisfaction to 78 percent from the previous 30 percent.

Truth, Not Motivational Speaking

People want the truth, no matter how good, bad, or ugly it is. Employees aren't stupid. They know the bad news already. They want to see if their leaders have the courage to acknowledge it.

The upper-level management of a large hotel in the gaming industry was dramatically changing the pay and structure of the casino floor. Management wouldn't talk openly about the obvious difficulties, which was the one thing the employees really cared about. Instead, management thought that a motivational speech would do the trick. The program failed.

Some managers don't realize that employees can see through upper management's intentions. One study found that only 47 percent believe management behaviors are consistent with the organization's values, and only 40 percent trust management always to communicate honestly.[2]

Throwing motivational speeches at people when what they need is honesty is ludicrous. Telling the truth, and not holding back, can rally people to move through the discomfort and push to the summit.

What are you holding back from your people?
What if they were strong enough to handle the truth?

Walk the Talk

Begin having leaders walk the talk and risk vulnerability. Can you bravely disclose the real problems in your organization? Can you demonstrate that it's okay to bring them up? Tell the truth about the things employees realize anyway. How many of the following themes do employees talk about secretly because they're not brave enough to declare them openly?

- *Your plan sucks.* If they think your current plan doesn't address the real issues or show the team how to win, you want them to say so.

- *Your team's weak.* Ineffectual leaders breed weak teams. Build a strong team, and maintain its strategic focus. Eradicate cowardice, arrogance, and incompetence. If these things exist, expose them. Experienced mountaineers know how to assess the teams they're leading. Who looks weak or needs more time summiting? Are they drinking enough water to avoid dehydration? How is their attitude? Do you have a system in place for monitoring your organization so that you can recognize the internal dangers?

- *You're too absorbed by operations.* Weak teams pull their leaders into operations. No team can implement a strategic plan without strength, unity, and focus. Start monitoring where management is spending its time. If they're getting pulled into operations, say something and fix it.

- *Your meetings are useless.* Fix your meetings. Your team is probably complaining about them already. Stop having meetings where only information is transferred and start having meetings where problems are surfaced and worked on and where group decisions are needed. (See Chapter Four on ideas for transforming your meetings.)

- *People are apathetic.* Apathy infects organizations at any time, and if it is not addressed, morale, productivity, and profits diminish. It's a hidden illness: you don't realize you have it until it's too late. It spreads from employee to employee, and only the most disciplined can stay motivated. Apathy comes easily in organizations with low altitude leaders. Consumed by selfish agendas and tool seduction, they breed followers who disrespect them or, worse, resign themselves to mediocrity. Once management creates an apathetic culture, it's a slippery slope down to the lowest levels of performance. Uninspired by leadership, employees ignore opportunities to improve. Poor quality, products lacking innovation, and grave customer service experiences commonly emerge from apathetic cultures. Mediocrity is the by-product of apathy.

Before you apply any of these methods, honestly assess your organizational culture. Can it handle people telling the truth? What's the level of turnover, workers' compensation, or employee lawsuits? Do they reflect deeper issues no one is brave enough to surface? How well do employees reveal what is left unsaid? (What they say after meetings is usually the real truth about how they feel.) How can you bring to the surface what is otherwise hidden?

With cowardice removed from your culture, will everyone be ready to move forward and change for the better? Actually, not quite. Another danger lurks ahead that can sacrifice your career or your team: being too comfortable.

Key Learnings

- Cowardice stops employees from challenging the status quo, holding others accountable and exposing weaknesses in the team.
- Unhooking cowardice requires bravery.
- Bravery can be induced by the constructive use of shame, truth, and walking the talk.

The South Face of Mount Shisha Pangma (26,289 feet)

Chris Warner

Danger #7

COMFORT

When I wonder what I'm doing up there, cold, exhausted and terrified, I remember the words of Winston Churchill: "When you are going through hell, keep going." He must have been a climber.
    —*Marie-Odile Meunier Bouchard,*
    climber and entrepreneur

Location: Mount Shisha Pangma, Tibet: The Second Attempt

In 2001, following our ascent and epic descent of Everest, my life entered a period of turmoil. I was emotionally beaten up by all the deaths and the stress of rescuing Andy and Jaime. When I came home, things were a mess. The press was treating me as a minor celebrity, which was an advantage to my business. But this just made it harder to deal with the mixed emotions of realizing my dream, at great expense. As the pressure built, I decided I needed to get back on the proverbial horse.

Three months after Everest, I was back on the crowded streets of Kathmandu. My plan was to return to Shisha Pangma, a mountain I had failed to climb in 1999. Now I wanted to try to climb it without any partners. It would be a lot more dangerous, with an ever-greater chance of failure. I figured that by fully immersing myself in a challenge of this magnitude and surrounding myself with that much risk, I would be forced to perform at my highest level of ability. I wanted to be so fully engaged that my self-confidence would rush back in, filling the void. (It seemed a lot more effective than any other type of therapy.)

On the trek to base camp, 9/11 occurred. During such an unfortunate and traumatic event, I felt blessed to be in a remote corner of the world.

My first attempt failed a few thousand feet up the face. Other teams were on the mountain, so I found a rarely climbed line, far to the right of them. After five hours of climbing, as I traversed some bulletproof ice, the pick on my ice ax broke. Useless, the tool dangled from my wrist while I hung by a second ax. The front points of my crampons were barely scratching the ice. I couldn't move up or sideways, and I was scared. If I sneezed, I'd die. I had to think fast and execute with perfection. My only choice was to rig a rope and descend the face. Nine rappels later, I arrived back on the glacier. I stumbled back to my tent, overcome by exhaustion and more than a bit disappointed by the failure, and I fell into a deep sleep.

I woke still committed to my goal, but not to that route. I came to Tibet to live fully, not to die. It seemed a lot safer to ascend a nearby route that a Korean team just finished. They had rigged 3,500 feet of rope on that part of the mountain, rope that I could use to descend if my ice ax broke again or for any other reason (like being scared out of my mind).

A few days later, I left my tent at 3:40 in the afternoon. I carried a small day pack, not big enough for a school kid but crammed with some water, snacks, a down jacket, and a video camera.

An extreme, challenging event lay before me: the first time any American climber made an unsupported ascent of one of the world's tallest peaks. Up until this time, American mountaineers climbed the biggest peaks in small or large groups. While summits were sometimes courageously made by solo American climbers leaving their buddies at some high camp, never before had they gone alone from bottom to top. This whole soloing game wasn't new to Himalayan mountaineering; it was just rare, and for a damned good reason.

To make matters even more challenging, I was to climb the whole mountain in a single push. I was on terrain completely new to me, without a tent, stove, sleeping bag, or other resources. I was committed to getting up and down without stopping.

Employing this style creates tremendous opportunity for failure. And it was just what I wanted. I was judging my success not by getting to the top but by being fully engaged in an intensive problem-solving initiative.

As darkness fell, I was nearly a thousand feet up the face. Soon I was above the height of the nearest peaks. Just behind them, the last gasps of the monsoon were pushing against the Himalayas. Storm clouds rolled up the valley systems, lightning flashing, rolling thunder crashing through the air. Light snowflakes whipped in the air around me. But overhead I could see stars. I knew that if the clouds pushed onto the mountain, I would have to retreat. There was no way, attached to the mountain by just my crampons or ice axes, I could survive a single avalanche.

The climbing was ridiculously difficult. The slopes were fifty to eighty degrees steep. To make things even more uncomfortable, a small rock band sliced across the route, just below midway. Climbing vertical rock just past midnight with temperatures far below freezing is risky. But I was feeling great, just as I had hoped to. Everything was coming together.

At 2:00 A.M. I puked. Carrying only two liters of water, with no means to melt more, this was an uncomfortable drawback. It meant that the level of dehydration I would suffer was far greater than I had anticipated. Dehydration at this altitude would increase my chances of becoming fatigued, affecting my cognitive abilities and inhibiting my body's ability to ward off frostbite. But as soon as I puked, I felt great.

I continued upward, engulfed in the darkness. After 6,000 feet of climbing, most of it standing and stepping from crampon point to crampon point, my calves were killing me. Can you imagine doing calf raises for nearly twelve hours? The pain became excruciating. I stopped to scream and really did feel better for doing it. I might be too proud to scream out loud in front of anyone, but alone it was a relief. I kept focusing on taking the next step. Just one more step.

Geoff, a transportation company CEO, had it all. He ran a successful business handed down from his parents, a great wife and kids, and enough cash and time to take a week of vacation every month. Now the competition was heating up, and he needed to do some serious work on his company. If he did it right, further regional expansion was possible.

In the weeks ahead, we started digging into the financials to see how the ratios were stacking up against the industry and assessing his business operations. The first thing we realized was that Geoff had to stop disappearing from the office every fourth week for a personal vacation. There were problems that required his attention. The deeper we dug, the more Geoff started getting irritated. One day when we asked what was going on, he threw a temper tantrum, "Why are we doing this? Why can't we just leave things the way they are?" All of these changes were threatening his cherished way of life, and suddenly Geoff became four years old. His scream wasn't a release of pain, freeing him to reach the summit; it was a cry of retreat. After we challenged him, it was clear he wasn't willing to avoid the danger that eats many leaders: comfort. We left. He muddled through.

Are you tempted to turn around when the journey becomes painful? How uncomfortable are you willing to be in order to get your career or team to the next level? Sure, minimizing risk and pain is comforting, and most aren't willing to take one more step when the going gets tough. But high altitude leaders want something more.

> Great achievements sometimes require
> enduring extreme discomfort.
> And that's when real leadership is tested,
> validated, and proven.

How Comfort Sabotages Your Greatness

Why do so many turn back when the going gets tough? Popular leadership trends easily seduce the unsophisticated when there's fine weather, an easy path, and plenty of air to breathe. You look like a genius when you have lots of cash, an abundance of time, and a simple agenda with minimal risk. As the saying goes, "Everyone is a great captain in calm seas." Only when the path ahead becomes formidable and risky, when certainty wavers and your legs quiver, does real greatness emerge—or not.

How easily are you distracted from important and vital decisions, especially when those decisions won't please others or will put you at risk? How badly do you want to reach the summit? When the avoidance of discomfort overcomes your leadership power, you can bet you'll give up summiting. We find comfort overtaking organizations at any altitude. Just look around at the employees. How many are:

- Practicing presenteeism, the opposite of absenteeism: retiring on the job, their journey to success degrading into just showing up?
- Seeing changes and accountability as just another excuse for victimization?
- Using corporate policies as a substitute for thinking?
- Making sure that "we've always done it that way" remains a valid excuse for not changing?
- Confusing activity with results?

Ever notice how big smiles and nodding heads in planning meetings become anguished faces when the team collides with the hard stuff? Unfortunately, many leaders find out too late that their people weren't saying, "Yes, I'm committed!" but instead, "I'm committed as long as it's fun, easy, and I don't have to sacrifice anything." Everybody's committed when it's comfortable. This explains why, in the face of daunting obstacles, companies often give up on their quests for greatness. They may have had an inspiring mission statement, but they didn't have a compelling saga to inspire them in the face of discomfort. Not everyone can achieve higher performance. Not everyone can continue to take just one more step.

> **There is nothing pleasurable, sexy, or exciting**
> **about taking just one more step**
> **when your body is totally aching and exhausted,**
> **but on the climb, it makes the critical difference**
> **between success and failure.**

The CEO of a marine services company knew it was time to battle the comfortable status quo and contacted us to help conduct a vital strategic planning session. He wanted to reposition the company, driving profit growth by 50 percent. Clearly the CEO knew the areas that needed to be confronted and dealt with. He presented the need for a strategy session to gain his executives' cooperation. That's when the walls went up:

"But we have a new data center going in!"
"We're moving the office this year."
"Why are we doing this?"
"Don't we already have a plan from a couple years ago?"

The race was lost before the gun went off. Operational demands once again sabotaged a strategic initiative. Couple this with a mistake some CEOs make, asking versus leading, and just wait to hear the sound of crushing metal as future success collides with walls of current reason. The CEO was far too weak to lead. He succumbed to the operational demands, not willing to be uncomfortable enough to challenge the status quo and the short-term urgencies. It was easier to avoid the real issues rather than take the one more step needed to push through the bad attitudes, exhaustion, disappointments, frustrations, and pain. The future was sacrificed on the altar of comfort.

Don't sacrifice your career on this altar. You grow only when you're putting yourself in uncomfortable positions and taking on new challenges. High performers are used to being uncomfortable. Many get nervous when things get too comfortable for too long.

> *The truth is that our finest moments are most likely to occur when we are feeling deeply uncomfortable, unhappy, or unfulfilled. For it is only in such moments, propelled by our discomfort, that we are likely to step out of our ruts and start searching for different ways or truer answers.*
>
> M. Scott Peck, American psychiatrist and author

Comfort's Evil Offspring: Politeness

Missed deadlines and mistakes revealed too late could be the result of a common, yet unspeakable, by-product of comfort. It secretly sacrifices performance and profits. It seduces managers to treat the symptoms while avoiding the real problems, to confuse activity with results, and to burn cash faster than the company can afford. It's unspeakable because it wouldn't be polite to mention it. And in that fact it reveals itself: a culture of politeness.

There's nothing wrong with politeness in society. It helped further the development of modern civilization. Robert Heinlein said, "For me, politeness is a sine qua non of civilization."[1] But in companies, politeness can emerge on the dark side by allowing people to do everything but the uncomfortable, essential act required for effective strategy and execution: tell the truth. Best said by Mary Wilson Little, "Politeness is only one half good manners and the other half good lying."[2] And in polite, comfortable cultures, you find more of the latter. In most teams, the only truths that are allowed to emerge are those that fit into a narrow realm of comfortable, safe, overused, and therefore ineffective forms of feedback; the rest are relegated to hushed tones in the restrooms and pubs after work.

Admit it: you've sat through many employee performance evaluations that were a total waste of time. Or certainly you can think of a dozen situations when the truth was glossed over because if it really came out, someone would be uncomfortable. But people and teams can't improve if you aren't giving them honest feedback about their weaknesses. Good leaders have to be honest to help those they lead develop.

After we had studied this pattern in hundreds of companies, one thing became clear:

> **Comfort promotes politeness.**
> **But politeness eats truth.**
> **And lack of truth eats profits.**

How do you know if politeness threatens your company? Answer these questions:

- Is avoiding discomfort by being nice more important than performing?
- Rather than revealing the uncomfortable truth about a situation, do people hide inside indirect politeness, only hinting at the problem?
- Are avoidance, denial, and silence preferred as opposed to confronting someone and risking pain, anger, retribution, and other unpleasantries?
- Do employees hide or only whisper about the uncomfortable issues, burying them within closed groups and hoping they will go away?

But surely, you may be thinking, *these things can't be that big of a threat. These are typical office behaviors. How much can they really hurt us?*

Collateral Damage from Comfort

Maintaining comfort in your company, your team, or yourself when you know that the right thing to do is take an uncomfortable step produces further injury and harm. The collateral damage from keeping the truth at unspeakable levels and preserving the status quo shows up in any number of ways.

Deadweight

Deadweight on your team prevents great people from assuming leadership. Comfort and politeness ensure policies are in place to keep mediocre performers on board. For example, one company in the technology service business was sliding lower in customer satisfaction scores and said they needed to clean house. We found out that most managers weren't willing to be uncomfortable enough to confront low performers immediately. In fact, the company policy was that five written warnings had to be issued before someone could be terminated. Deadweight just kept piling up.

In another case, a chemical process company manager, Chuck, couldn't take it anymore: Sam, a production employee, had to leave. He always had a bad attitude on the job, and it was starting to cause quality problems on the line. Chuck raged at human resources (HR) because the department wasn't moving fast enough on terminations. The problem was that when HR checked the employee's file, they found that Sam's direct supervisor had given him stellar reviews. When asked why, the supervisor replied, "Well, I didn't want to hurt his feelings." The supervisor was too uncomfortable to give Sam the honest feedback he so desperately needed.

Now the company has a weight problem and a "wait" problem: HR needs time for several cycles of employee reviews in order to avoid a lawsuit.

Phantom Leadership

Who are the real leaders your people follow? Many programs get stalled because the managers on the organization chart aren't the people the employees are following. Instead, the people are following phantom leaders: the informal leaders whom management never appointed to lead the group. This is not a problem in itself, but it can be a catastrophe if the phantom leader is going in the wrong direction. So when formal leaders declare an initiative, they may have no idea that their people are really listening to someone else. And when that happens, the initiative stalls. Management then tries to figure out what went wrong, but no one exposes the problem. It would be too uncomfortable.

A manufacturing company CEO was delighted to finally unleash a new quality program that entailed teamwork and productivity improvements on the plant floor. Everyone applauded. In the cafeteria, Joe, a high-seniority employee, called his fellow workers together and informed them, "That all sounds nice. But these things blow over. Don't worry. We're gonna keep our overtime. We know how to throttle the line speed." Everyone nodded.

Another example is a health care system we worked with. Management was frustrated with years of chronic delays and faltering change programs. During a management conference, we asked the sponsoring executive if she wanted to take a risk and finally get at the root of the problem. She was hesitant but agreed. We then introduced an exercise whereby everyone was able to disclose whose leadership they really followed.

> The truth will set you free. But first, it will piss you off.
>
> Gloria Steinem

The result? Upper management discovered that the leaders people were really following weren't the ones on the organization chart. This explained a lot.

The formal managers were hurt and angry. In the end, the gloves came off: people started telling the uncomfortable truth, revealing bottlenecks, and exposing accountability issues. Of

Location: Shisha Pangma, continued

After my screaming fit, I continued upward. Dawn caught me just below the summit ridge. For the first time in fifteen hours, I found a place to sit down. I was physically tired but emotionally wound up. I didn't sit for long. At 9:00 A.M. I was on the summit, seventeen hours and twenty minutes after starting. The views were magical. From my perch, I could see eight of the world's tallest peaks, with thousands more scattered beneath them. To the east rose Everest, Cho Oyu, Lhotse, Makalu, and Kanchenjunga. To the south and west stood Annapurna, Manaslu, and Dhualagiri. To the north, the Tibetan plateau stretched to Mongolia, with just the hallowed Mount Kailash, source of some of Asia's longest rivers (the Indus and Bhramaputra), rising above the barren brown plains.

I started the descent thinking that I would be safely on the ground by late afternoon. Around midday, the exhaustion, altitude, and dehydration caught up with me. Their combined effect manifested itself in a very strange way. I was lying on the slope, my feet kicked into my old footsteps, my ice axes plunged into the snow, my wrists locked to thin loops of webbing running from the shafts of the axes.

I was above 26,000 feet and in the death zone, and I started hallucinating. I suddenly had the feeling that I was escorted across this section of the mountain on my way up. And sure enough, when I looked to the right side of the wide gully, I could see a dozen hobbits scrambling among the rocks. I yelled over to Bilbo Baggins, asking for help.

"I won't come and get you," he hollered back.

"But why?"

"Because you threw Gandalf in jail."

"But that was years ago!"

I was convinced that I couldn't cross this section alone. If someone didn't come for me, I would die. I clung to the axes to wait. It slowly dawned on me that all this was a dream. I was never helped across this section. I needed to descend the mountain on my own.

I was climbing down fifty- to sixty-degree slopes, searching for the topmost rope left by the Koreans. I couldn't remember where the ropes were, since the route I ascended only vaguely paralleled that of the Koreans, most often following the path of least resistance. I just knew that at some point, the ropes would begin, and I'd find them on the right wall of the gully.

The gully varied in width from a dozen to a few hundred feet. Still hallucinating, I gave up waiting for the hobbits, accepted whatever fate awaited, and traversed the gully. At the far side I saw an old trailer home, with a guy in cutoff jeans and a white tank top sitting on the porch.

"Hey, mister, do you know where I can find the fixed lines?"

"They aren't in yet. We're not putting them in until the Ozzie Osbourne concert."

"When will that be?"

"In a few weeks."

I remember thinking that I couldn't afford to wait for weeks. I figured I had traversed right too soon, so set off again, crisscrossing back left across the slopes. In the end, I completed seven legs of a Z, trying to find those ropes. And I found them not a second too soon. It was now dark and snowing. Loose powder avalanches started to pour, like tipped dump trucks of coarse sugar, down the gully system. I clipped into the ropes and started an endless series of rappels. Two hours later, the snow stopped, and with it the avalanches eased off. At 9:00 P.M. I unclipped from the last rappel. At 10:40 P.M. I arrived back at my tent. Three months after guiding clients to the summit of Mount Everest, I had climbed Shisha Pangma just for me.

As a leader, you often won't have all the tools, resources, or circumstances you need, yet you still must summit. Perseverance separates the high altitude leaders from the charlatans. Business history is rich with such examples—there are many Edisons who persevered through hundreds of failures in order to create the right lightbulb—yet this passion to persevere appears lacking in many of today's business organizations. No team or professional accomplishes a goal worth the pursuit without surviving the stretch—the often uncomfortable and at times painful stretch—called *perseverance.*

In 1990, Chris was working for Outward Bound, training staff and running wilderness courses. There was a real mix of clients, from spoiled to incarcerated kids. Chris and his staff were also running team-building programs for corporate groups. One week, they'd have the sheriff take the handcuffs off kids at the start of the course, and the next they'd be at the Aspen Institute watching senior vice presidents build bridges from boards and parade around with blindfolds. Chris was having a lot of fun, but the work wasn't that challenging. At the end of the year, he went off to Ama Dablam, a beautiful peak in Nepal. A friend and he survived a winter ascent of the West Face, completing what was described as the hardest climb done in the Himalayas that season.

When he came back to work, Chris grew restless. By September 1990, he needed a change. He wanted to break away from Outward Bound and teach rock climbing full-time. Chris had been teaching classes in his spare time but couldn't figure out how to make a living doing it. A co-instructor looked him in the eye one day and laid out the harsh truth: "Why are you so willing to take such extreme personal risks but act like a coward when it comes to taking a professional risk?"

He was right. Chris was too comfortable in his safe job to take a risk. He was willing to let his dream die without giving it a chance. Chris survived cowardice because his co-instructor shamed him into bravery. Chris quit his job at Outward Bound to start Earth Treks. He scraped together every penny he could find, and with $592 in the bank, Earth Treks was officially in business. Those early years were lean. He was on the road constantly, running as many trips as he could.

In 1995, Chris was guiding in Boulder, Colorado, and noticed that most of the local guide services had been forced out of business by a new threat: the indoor climbing gym. Climbing guides had all snickered when these first opened: Why would anyone pay to climb indoors when the real adventure took place on remote and scary cliffs? The joke, though, was on them. People fell in love with the convenience and sense of community that the gyms offered. Gyms were popping up all around the country, with two in Chris's own state.

The writing was on the wall. Chris either had to give up his dream or find a way to open a gym. A few weeks later he found a way in a stormbound tent at 14,000 feet on a peak in Alaska. Chris remembers it clearly:

> Kevin Maloney and I were climbing Mount McKinley. Midway up the mountain, we were caught in a storm that raged on for six days. We just lay in our sleeping bags, shifting every few hours to ease the pain in our hips. The boredom was so mind-numbing that I started to mumble out loud about this idea of opening a gym.
>
> Maloney is a smart guy, and even though he was just thirty-six at the time, he was a battle-hardened businessman. He had been a banker, but during the savings and loan crisis of the early 1990s, he bailed on the lending side to become a borrower. He saw properties in Manhattan being sold at tremendous discounts and wanted to find a way to capitalize on that once-in-a-career opportunity. For months at a time, he slept on friends' floors, operated his business from a folding table, and scraped together a portfolio of distressed properties that was worth nearly $1 billion.
>
> The only paper we had with us was toilet paper. With a marker and long strips of toilet paper laid on the floor of the tent, we worked on the projections. It was the perfect distraction to

the endless blizzard. We never summited the mountain. By the time the storm ended, the snow was so deep that all the teams headed home.

A few weeks later, Kevin sent me a little package with $20,000 in it. By the time the gym was built, he had sent me $400,000 more. What Maloney didn't tell me was that building out that gym was going to be the toughest adventure that I'll ever embark on, making mountaineering seem like a vacation. An Everest expedition takes ten weeks. It took us over eighteen months to open that first gym. The first battle was securing the financing, and Maloney attached some strict rules to the loan: I had to pay him back within five years of opening. The interest rate was reflective of the risk. He insisted that we become the general contractor and that very little of the construction could be subcontracted. He wanted to see us convert the $400,000 into a facility worth twice as much. He had built his real estate business this way, and he wanted me to do the same.

When he told me he'd fund the gym, Earth Treks had two full-time employees (we were both climbing bums) and a handful of part-timers. Our gross income was less than $100,000 a year. We ran the business from a spare bedroom in the old house I was renting. We were struggling in our efforts to operate a climbing school in one of America's flattest states, Maryland; now we were faced with hiring a team and building the gym, negotiating leases, purchasing computers and software systems, developing a retail store, and figuring out how to run a totally new kind of business, one that none of us had any practical experience with.

It took us ten months to find a building (we needed ceiling heights of at least forty feet and in a suburban, retail-friendly location). We spent another two months negotiating the leases, getting building permits, and dealing with other preconstruction tasks. Finally in June 1996, we started construction. We thought we would open the gym in October. But Christmas came and went, and we were still building the climbing walls. We were now out of money, begging Maloney to send us some more cash so we could buy more nails and two-by-fours.

The more desperate things seemed from a financial standpoint, the more the team building the walls rallied. We loved having the odds pile up against us. We were living out our compelling saga. We were an entrepreneurial David facing Goliath, and we knew the final steps to the summit are the most exhausting. We announced to the climbing world that the gym was opening at 3:00 P.M. on January 29, 1997. In the last three weeks before that date, we never left the building. We worked until we dropped, slept for two or three hours every night, and then got up and worked more.

At midnight on January 28, we sprayed the last of the textured paint on the wall. At dawn, we scraped the floors clean, mopped the bathrooms, and drove the scissor lifts out of the building. At noon, the final building inspection was completed. And at 2:45 P.M., we finished laying the padding on the floor.

None of us had ever worked a cash register. We didn't even know how much money we needed to put in the cash drawer to make change. But, hey, a few months earlier, we didn't know how to apply for a building permit, negotiate a lease, or install a sprinkler system.

At 3:00 P.M. when I unlocked the door, I saw over a hundred climbers lined up on the sidewalk to get in. A few months after opening that gym, the national Climbing Gym Association published its survey of the nation's more than one hundred commercial climbing gyms. We had only eight months of data to provide the association, while our peers sent in their figures for the full twelve months, but still we were listed as the sixth-highest-grossing gym in the country.

It still amazes me that Maloney lent us that money. I didn't know a thing about operating a business of the size and complexity of what we now have. The only thing I knew how to do was to climb big mountains. Every time I called him, he'd say: "Run your business like you run your expeditions, and you'll reach the summit." So we did. We chose a nearly impossible goal. We built a team that was passionate about reaching that goal, and we persevered until we reached the top.

Wizened by the process of building three gyms now and from all the time we've spent with other CEOs, we can tell you with certainty that a compelling saga will drive passion for your strategy, but the uncomfortable, unsexy, simplistic concept of perseverance will drive your execution. If you build a team that loves to work hard, you'll outexecute your competition every time.

Why are stories of entrepreneurs overcoming thousands of rejections, or overwhelming challenges, in their never-ending journey to enduring success retold in folktale ways? These stories offer universal appeal. Most of us don't possess any special talents or an atmospheric IQ. But we do show up for work every day and give it our best effort. A business school student summed it up perfectly after listening to a presentation that Chris had just delivered: "Thanks for finally letting me know that you don't have to be smart to be successful."

If you've been at this game for any length of time, you've experienced failure. In the natural course of life, your heart will be broken, your team will lose games, and your attempts to climb higher will fail. Instead of stopping, high altitude leaders become greater as a result. Great literature builds on this simple premise: conflicts result in character development. You are the main character in this story, and you will grow to your potential only by going through big and small conflicts. If you avoid the conflicts or dwell on the associated pain, you will not grow. Pity your bad fortune, and your book becomes so miserable that no one will waste time reading it. But persevere, and there's no telling what you can summit.

But what is perseverance? The dictionary defines it as the "steady persistence in a course of action, a purpose, a state, etc., esp. in spite of difficulties, obstacles, or discouragement." Simple enough. But before you persevere for a goal, make sure you know the difference between perseverance and blind persistence.

Blind Persistence Is Not Perseverance

Location: Mount Shisha Pangma, Tibet—First Attempt

On a snowy day in October 1999, my partner and I arrived at a remote Tibetan base camp. Shisha Pangma is the fourteenth-tallest mountain in the world. We were headed for the South Face, an extremely technical, rarely climbed objective on this 26,289-foot-tall mountain. Some of the best mountaineers in the world had tried this face, and it seemed like a fitting challenge to us. After all, we had just survived a climb of Cho Oyu, the world's sixth-highest peak. It had been a rather maturing season so far. On Cho Oyu, I was swept up in a massive avalanche, only to be cast aside just seconds before it launched off a cliff face. And constant storms battered the mountain, allowing only forty of the more than three hundred climbers to reach the top.

Two other teams were already on Shisha Pangma. A dozen or so Eastern European climbers were in base camp, and nine Americans, filming a TV show, were at advanced base camp. That day the snows stopped, and the sun popped out for the first time in many days. Above us the winds were still howling, with clawlike lenticular clouds forming over the summit. You may have never seen a lenticular cloud, which forms most often in the mountains. These ominous clouds are a sign of superhigh winds blowing at altitude.

Seduced by the sunlight, the American team left their tents at advanced base camp. They hoped to recon a route to the base of the mountain and maybe shoot some film. Six members of the team stuck to the rock, and three headed on to the glacier. It seemed innocent enough.

But high above them, the winds and recent snows were interacting with the force of gravity. A small avalanche cut free from near the summit. As it traveled down the face, it triggered an ever wider avalanche that eventually bisected the entire face. Hundreds of thousands of pounds of ice and rock fell at breakneck speeds, crashing onto the glacier.

The climbers on the glacier ran for their lives. One climber headed across the slope, and the others went straight downhill. The avalanche struck. Two climbers were killed, then buried beneath thousands of tons of ice and snow. The third was tossed and battered, dislocating his shoulder, but he survived.

Late that night, a frantic Sherpa, working with the American team, ran into our camp and told us the tragic news. We recruited the Eastern European team, and before first light, we were all on our way to the advanced base camp to help in any way we could.

It snowed all that day and the next. We were all struck with grief. It was hard to lose two such magnificent men and such experienced climbers. We chiseled their names into slabs of rock and gathered for a ceremonial good-bye.

My partner and I chose to abandon the climb. It was clearly too dangerous. That storm system, by the time it finished crossing the Himalayas, claimed the lives of thirteen climbers on three different mountains. A dozen expeditions lost their gear and abandoned their dreams. It cost us a few thousand dollars to walk away from Shisha Pangma, and we never even touched the mountain.

I will never forget looking back at the South Face of Shisha Pangma. The view was intoxicating, the climbing possibilities awe inspiring. If there was ever something to be passionate about as a mountaineer, surely it is that face of that mountain.

How many times do you hold on to a dream too hard? Still pursue a project you've already sunk too much time and money into? Let the ego rather than the head drive the agenda? Can you walk away as we did? We had spent thousands of dollars to reach the base of that mountain, yet we walked away. And sometimes you may need to do the same.

Retreating does not mean giving up or lacking perseverance. This flies in the face of many trendy leadership theories that inspire you always to be out in front, always on top:

- "The view always looks the same unless you're the lead dog."
- "Quitters never win, and winners never quit."
- "If you can't play with the big dogs, stay on the porch."

Yadda yadda yadda. A problem surfaces when experts and motivational speakers who tout these insights never see the damage they do. They're missing in action when a believer continues onward long after he or she should have retreated. In fact, many of these motivational speakers probably never ran a dogsled team. Every year we run sleds with dogs training for the Iditarod race. Contrary to the above quotation, the view is never the same for the dogs following the lead dogs. We can never get these dogs to line up. They're always bouncing along, looking out to the sides, or nipping at each other. The poor lead dogs have the toughest job: trying to pull everyone straight forward on the trail.

So, sure, we could have attempted Shisha Pangma that season. But chances are we would've died trying, and a leader can't ignore reality. Retreat, not blind persistence, can sometimes be the only course of action.

The emotional cost of retreat can be severe, however. Your self-confidence gets bruised. You feel weaker, maybe even lapse into depression. Comfort totally eludes you. But high altitude leaders don't seek comfort in denying or rationalizing why it happened, as seductive as that comfort can be. Instead, they accept what happened while not losing faith in the compelling saga that drives them. Walking away does not mean giving up. It's about maintaining a higher-level strategy that allows you to withdraw and then return again. It's not a sign of weakness; only smart leaders know when and how to retreat well.

> **Perseverance does not mean continuing on in the
> face of impossible obstacles,
> but having the capacity to retreat, rethink, and return.**

How to Inspire Perseverance

Perseverance takes more than a bunch of positive affirmations to keep going. The danger of comfort remains ever present, manifesting itself as excessive politeness, contentment, or even laziness. If you suspect that your team suffers from this, there's a way out. In leading hundreds of groups past their comfort zone, we've found that the following ideas provide a journey worth taking.

Reveal the Truth, Not Motivational Posters

Many times managers fail to inspire their people to persevere in the face of being stopped. They mistakenly focus on motivational speeches and posters to get people past the hard stuff. But people really want something more. They want the truth, no matter how hard it may sound. Avoiding the truth or covering it up with speeches only engenders distrust in an organization. In our work with teams in the most harrowing situations, we find that perseverance doesn't come from transparent manipulative techniques in order to achieve greatness. Given a clear goal, people can handle the truth and exceed their own perceived limitations.

> **In leadership, as in climbing, the higher you go,
> the greater the challenges become.
> Get used to telling the truth.**

Warn your team about the trials ahead. If they know what to expect, they can battle discomfort with a positive mental attitude. Perseverance requires personal sacrifice, and nobody willingly engages in sacrifice without a compelling set of reasons. Challenge your team and yourself to face the truth and be uncomfortable, to relinquish comfort for the possibility of a greater cause. On the mountain face, the prospect of death is that reason, but what about in the business environment? A good leader inspires perseverance for a greater cause with a compelling saga that drives people to higher results over their tendencies for comfort and politeness. If comfort seduces you to hold back and resist change, just remember that no one wants to follow a has-been. If you aren't moving your industry forward by setting a pioneering path for your company, how can you expect your team to persevere toward lofty goals? Great professionals and teams endure whatever suffering and pain they must in order to reach the new future they are creating.

One word of warning: putting your own selfish needs above your saga brings perseverance to a deadly stop. So avoid any intention of self-gain, career growth, or even trappings of material success. No one is waking up in the morning wondering how to make you more important or richer. Sam Walton drove a battered old pickup, and Warren Buffett lives in the same small house he bought over thirty years ago. No excuses for you.

As soon as Chris returned from the summit of Shisha Pangma to the United States, he gathered the Earth Treks team together. The world had changed that year: the dot-com bubble had crashed, and the ripple effects of 9/11 had reached his core business. (No one needed any more adventure in their lives, so business slowed at both the climbing gym and international mountaineering expeditions.) He could have tried to avoid the real issue, but when faced with the truth, his team saw all of this as an opportunity to take a corporate risk. The commercial real estate market was contracting, with rental rates dropping back into the range an indoor climbing gym could afford. It was time for Earth Treks to expand. Chris was fresh off the summit of one mountain, and his team wanted to embark on a new adventure. It was time to build a new gym, effectively doubling the size of his business.

Warning: If the gap between here and there becomes so large for your team that staying where they are turns out to be more comfortable, you've got a problem. If your team is unwilling to persevere, best to find out earlier rather than later. And if you're not the CEO or someone who can transform the company culture, submit your resignation and get a job with a company that needs your leadership.

Just Take One More Step

Telling the truth does something else: it prepares people to keep going even when they hit the wall. It's precisely when your confidence eludes you, when your physical and emotional capacity dries up, that you need to take one more step, then another, and another. When leading teams in this situation, high altitude leaders lead by example.

But what about the lack of confidence when people hit the wall? Don't they need confidence to keep going? The answers are sometimes counterintuitive. For example, many popular approaches to business management encourage an emphasis on fostering confidence among a team's members. But success requires perseverance in the face of continued obstacles or failures, even if one's confidence fails. Just as mountain climbers exert superhuman effort to save life and limb even when they feel worthless in the face of seemingly insurmountable obstacles, high altitude leaders also persevere through the most difficult business circumstances.

Chris had this impact on Don when he climbed Cotopaxi in Ecuador. Don remembers it this way:

> When we climbed Cotopaxi with Chris, it was the most challenging climb I'd ever done. It was probably just another day at the office for seasoned mountaineers like Chris, but I had not climbed for over fifteen years since my wife, Mary, and I trekked through the Himalayan mountains of Bhutan (then

we had kids and our expeditions stopped). It took four months of training, and the loss of seventeen pounds of body fat, to get into reasonable enough shape even to attempt this summit. Still, I was challenged by the mountain. Cotopaxi is the world's highest active volcano, and volcanoes grow like a funnel, so the climb only gets steeper as you go up.

We started climbing the final summit at midnight. By 4:00 A.M. I was ready to turn around like many teams had done before. The temperature had dipped below zero, the slope neared fifty degrees, and the crevasses that sliced across the glacier seemed bottomless. As I climbed through the night with just a little headlamp to illuminate the way, each ridge brought hope, but then despair, as another vertical ascent appeared in the distance.

I remember seeing bright stars high in the night sky, and they were moving! Later I realized they were the headlamps of teams that had left earlier. The summit seemed like an endless and hopeless journey, further removing itself from my grasp on each small ledge we reached.

Then things got worse. My partner started vomiting at 18,000 feet, not uncommon at high altitudes due to the lack of oxygen. I started getting nauseous hearing him vomit but couldn't get away because we were roped together. Sick and exhausted, we still had several hours of climbing ahead. But we continued. Each step I took was a major effort, requiring several breaths before mustering up enough energy for the next one. I lost my motivation. I lost confidence. But something kept me going.

What kept me going?

I remembered Chris's warnings all too well: the biggest challenge wouldn't be physical but emotional. He told us how grueling and uncomfortable it was going to be. No motivational speech was going to con us into thinking it was going to be easy. Chris calculated almost to the foot at what altitude the team would be feeling doubt and despair, when the reality of the challenge would exceed their passion. He knew we would consider pulling back and giving up. "That's the time," he said, "to keep going. Take the pain and the discomfort with you onward and upward. Just keep taking one more step." Chris coached us many times preparing us for that moment. Rather than avoiding the truth and resorting to some motivational speech, he made us face the uncomfortable reality ahead. A motivational speech would've seemed like a contrived attempt at manipulation. He geared us up for meeting that challenge with one simple action: continue moving forward, and take one more step.

Chris's coaching prepared me for the uncomfortable moments. The self-doubt wasn't unexpected. I had been warned it would happen. But we summited after seven and a half hours, nearly twice the time it would take me to run a marathon. I'll never forget the exhilaration of it all.

Paradoxically, business leaders are not trained this way. They aren't taught to tell their team that self-doubt and pain are certainties. Wouldn't it be easier for the team to persevere if they knew that the agony they are dealing with is normal? Why is it that coaches are given permission by athletes to lead them through painful practices and brutal games, but business leaders quiver in front of their employees when a task gets too challenging?

> **Rest rarely comes to those seeking the
> next level of performance.
> Perseverance jump-starts the climb when all
> momentum seems lost.**

Cut Off Deadweight

Remember the damage that comfort causes by allowing the buildup of deadweight in the organization? People have higher levels of perseverance if they're not handicapped by deadweight. It's the difference between summiting with a day pack or a yak on your back. People persevere better alongside those they respect. Of course, confronting deadweight behaviors isn't comfortable, but neither is the failure that results from avoiding accountability. So look at your policies and work to create fair systems that enable you to deal effectively with the deadweight that stalls performance. Then train your managers on how to use the new policies and be authentic with their staff.

Once you start removing deadweight, your best employees will be happier (while the losers will start to flee in a state of panic). Great people want to work with other great people and to know that management notices what they contribute. This tactic works well at GE, Earth Treks, and hundreds of other companies. Teams that engage in life-or-death challenges, as well as CEOs like GE's former legendary CEO Jack Welsh, know that weak teammates will kill you. Your survival, and ultimately your excellence, depend on culling the weak.

Align the Phantoms

Enhance perseverance by aligning the phantom leaders in your organization. Companies that ignore phantom leadership get nowhere fast, especially when these leaders are inspiring the team in directions that conflict with the corporation's goals. Have you cultivated the right talent by identifying the real champions in your company—the people who can really lead? These champions don't have to be technically competent, but they must be able to inspire others to follow them toward where the organization wants to go. Does your company know how to select those leaders? Does it invest the time and money to train those with the appropriate leadership skills?

If you ever identify a negative phantom leader, get rid of that person instantly. Otherwise he or she will destroy you. We've tried all sorts of techniques to win these folks over, from giving them groups to lead, to pulling them aside in an effort to get them to work for the greater good, to challenging them in public. In our opinion, all of these techniques are a waste of time and emotional energy. Negative phantom leaders are leeches that become stronger as they suck your organization's blood. Don't let them pack their own things when they leave; ship the things to them. (Many managers find phantom leaders stealing as they leave the company.)

Finally, the most critical challenge may not be when you've successfully persevered and summited but what happens next. Comfort always seeks a way into your life and your company's life. Its best opportunity to strike occurs when perseverance is no longer necessary. How many companies have been contaminated with status quo cultures after their heroic journey to the top?

After the greatest of companies have successfully achieved lofty goals, the comfort of status quo consumes them.

But even if you do it all correctly, there are no guarantees of success. Embracing death, having a compelling saga, focusing on behavior and adaptation, seeking humility, partnership, bravery, and perseverance certainly ensure you avoid many dangers. But the last danger is the culprit that kills every climber and high altitude leader who did everything right: gravity.

Key Learnings

- Comfort sabotages the pursuit of a compelling saga.
- Comfort breeds politeness, contentment, and laziness; and politeness eats profits.
- Don't lead if you lack the willingness to be uncomfortable.
- Perseverance sometimes requires retreat.
- Beware of success after perseverance, lest comfort finds you again.

Dan Jenkins jumping a crevasse

Chris Warner

Danger #8

GRAVITY

We can lick gravity, but the paperwork's a bit tougher.

—*Werner von Braun, rocket scientist*

Location: K2, Pakistan

The trek to K2's base camp follows a twisting valley for seven days and sixty-five miles. The trail starts at 7,000 feet and is hot and dusty as it leaves the last village. Traveling with us are 120 porters, each carrying fifty-five pounds of expedition equipment and food. We have supplies to last us for seventy days. Twenty-five miles (and three days) into the journey, we leave the hot trails and step onto the Baltoro Glacier, one of the longest glaciers in the world. Beneath our feet, the ice varies in thickness from 600 to 1,200 feet. And all of this ice is slowly sliding down valley.

Glaciers move with the terrain, bending around corners and tumbling over cliffs. The outer layer is brittle, like the chocolate coating of a Snickers bar. And the inside is easily deformed, like the caramel and nougat filling. Bend a Snicker's bar, and it resembles a glacier. The cracks are the crevasses, and the islands of chocolate are seracs. On a glacier, those crevasses are hundreds of feet deep, and the seracs (upthrust chunks of glacial ice) can tower more than 100 feet above you.

The worst accident in North American mountaineering involved a collapsing serac. All eleven victims are still buried beneath the rubble, even though the accident happened nearly twenty-five years ago. Fall into a crevasse unroped, and you may never be seen again. Most crevasses are jagged cracks, with the walls eventually squeezing together. Fall through a 10-foot-wide crevasse, and some 200 feet later, you'll be wedged into place, like a cork. Exhale, and your suddenly smaller chest allows you to slip an inch or two deeper. Luckily the temperatures are well below freezing, so you'll soon be hypothermic. In the Alps, they might be able to get you out with the help of a jackhammer. But in the remote corners of the world, you will freeze to death.

We walk for four days on the surface of the Baltoro and, later, the Godwin Austin glacier. Between 10,000 and 17,200 feet, the glacier is covered by a thin veneer of rock called moraine. Base camp is on the very last stretch of this moraine. All that rubble effectively fills in the crevasses, and the dangers of a serac collapse or a crevasse fall below base camp are negligible.

We arrived in base camp on June 1. Early the next morning, Bruce Normand and Don Bowie set off on the glacier, reconning a route to K2's East Face. Within an hour, they started to encounter crevasses, then seracs and marked the dangers with bamboo wands. Tied to each other by forty feet of climbing rope, they watched each other carefully as they hopped over the crevasses. It would be impossible to count the number of crevasses they saw.

No one had been up that glacier in years. There was no obvious route, just a half-mile-wide glacier, flat in places, rolling in others, and occasionally crushed into an "icefall," where it flowed over a cliff. In the early afternoon, about three miles from base camp, they crested a slight rise and found themselves on a nearly flat plateau. With clouds forming and a light snow falling, they planted the last bamboo wand and returned to camp.

They passed a body along the way. This climber had been avalanched off the mountain many years ago and swept into a crevasse. Once trapped in the glacier, the body is frozen in place. The movement of the glacier is like a conveyor belt, slowly pushing the person to the surface, perhaps a mile or so down valley. Usually the body is dismembered, and perhaps just an arm or leg will surface. This time the torso was pushed out and now lay on top.

Very few of the climbers who die on K2 can be carried out. Normally they die high on the peak. On Everest, where it isn't too steep, the bodies lie in place. On K2, it is just too steep. All the bodies eventually avalanche off and become entombed in the glacier. In 2002, when I was first attempting K2, the remains of Dudley Wolfe were found. He was the first person to die on the mountain, back in 1939.

It snowed all night. Before dawn, Bruce and I were headed back up the glacier, hoping to push the route across the glacier to a place we had marked on satellite pictures. It would be our advanced base camp. From here, we would climb the mountain's East Face, one of the last great challenges on K2.

Six inches of snow hid Bruce and Don's day-old footsteps. But we could see the bamboo wands, and Bruce knew the way. We walked right past the torso, climbed through the icefall, and watched as the sun rose. On our left rose K2, the world's second-tallest peak. On our right was Broad Peak, the twelfth-tallest mountain. Straight ahead was a horseshoe-shaped valley formed by a twisted ridgeline spiked by a dozen 23,000- to 25,000-foot peaks. These peaks formed the border between Pakistan and China.

We were in one of the most remote corners of the world, seventy miles from the nearest road, hundreds of miles from the nearest hospital, and thirteen thousand miles from home. A few hundred feet away was the last of the bamboo wands. Soon we would be on untrodden terrain. But right here, Bruce and Don had passed just a day before.

The fresh snow covered the glacier's icy surface. Like snowfall on a parking lot, it was perfectly flat. Bruce was in the lead, leaving neat footprints in the snow. We were fifty feet apart, tied by fifty-five feet of rope. The rope was snug but not quite tight. Despite the glacier being flat, we knew there were crevasses in this area. We stepped carefully and took all the normal precautions. When we did find a crevasse, the climber in the lead would probe the edges with his ice ax, and once we knew where the edge was, we would hop from one side to the other. All of this is standard practice. We had probably hopped over fifty crevasses so far this morning.

Not every crevasse appears as a gaping hole or a jagged crack. Sometimes the walls of the crevasse are bridged by a thick layer of snow. If these snow bridges are thick enough, we walk across them. On Everest, where the crevasses grow to twenty or thirty feet wide, we lay sections of ladders across, forming the scariest bridge you'll ever cross. Stepping from ladder rung to ladder rung, you are forced to look at your feet and into the ever-darker void below.

Traveling on a glacier is not for the faint of heart.

Between us and the bamboo wand, the glacier was perfectly flat, and the fresh layer of snow hid any dangers. Bruce took another step.

He disappeared.

Get used to one simple fact: high altitude leadership is an endless journey full of risk. You constantly tread in unfamiliar areas. Although plans are made and experts say the path is clear, you still may fall, and fall hard. Assumptions prove to be erroneous, data end up being flawed, or commitments go unmet. All of a sudden, a cherished project, career move, or critical goal appears to reach a point of failure, as it did for those who made these comments:

- "I knew the sales target was a stretch, but it was doable. I didn't know that the market wouldn't see the value in this new service."
- "We thought we had that client in the bag. When they went to a competitor, it was a total shock. We're still reeling from the effects."
- "I was counting on that promotion. But then the merger happened. That's when my career plans went sideways."
- "The supply chain was all set, and then the dollar went south. Now we're left holding the bag. Our pricing strategy is set to fail. We'll never make a profit on this product."

As high altitude leaders, we choose to climb big peaks, and lots of them. The higher those peaks are in both our professional and personal lives, the more some mysterious force tries to pull us down. Welcome to your final danger: gravity.

Gravity: The Great Equalizer

All sorts of gravitational forces haunt you in the world. When gravity propels you, you seem invincible. When it's pulling you down, you fall hard. In business, gravity emerges as that mysterious force of uncertainty that unpredictably pushes or pulls you for no apparent reason. In the late 1990s, it seemed that anyone with a computer was able to start an Internet company. Some even had the chutzpah to engineer an initial public offering before they even had a product. It was silly money chasing stupid ideas. The gravitational force propelled the market so powerfully that a lot of people got fabulously rich. Then one day in March 2001, gravity decided to reverse itself, and the bubble burst. A few cashed out and stuck others with the stock, but most investors lost millions. The last genius, as he turned out the lights, realized he wasn't so smart after all. The dot-com bubble crash left in its wake a loss of $7 trillion in fictitious value.[1]

More recently a lot of us benefited from the rising housing market. Our houses increased in value while we did nothing. If you were too lazy to get caught up in the excitement of flipping houses and too busy to partake in the insatiable greed of subprime lending, then you probably just bought a house before things went crazy and watched your property increase in value. Yes, you may have lost some of the gains, but your asset still appreciated at greater than historical rates until the gravity shifted.

Are we saying that what makes a company look great or bad may be more a matter of gravity's shift than any management technique?

Exactly.

Why do you think companies so quickly rotate off the Top 10 Greatest Companies lists published every year? Some even go bankrupt. Phil Rosenzweig's research gives us clues to this effect. Contrary to the opinions of all the books about what makes a company great, Rosenzweig's *The Halo Effect* shows how little we really know about how a company becomes successful.[2] For example, if a company expands and is successful, we say that its leaders were smart to diversify and extend their products; if the company fails, we say they drifted away from their core focus. But these divergent opinions end up applying to companies in the same industry, or even the same company! Rosenzweig uses great examples tracking the expert and media opinions of companies like Lego, WH Smith, Cisco, and ABB, and how opinions about the management methods of these companies changed depending on whether their stock price was going up or down. One moment the professors, consultants, and journalists were raving about the brilliance of the CEO; then when the stock price fell, they picked them apart for doing all the wrong things. In the end, you have confused CEOs scratching their heads wondering what happened, because they hadn't done anything differently. One day the strategy looked great; the next day it looked awful. Nothing changed except for the opinions and the weather. Picking through the delusions, Rosenzweig concludes that thinking we can control outcomes is tenuous; strategy and execution involve too much risk and uncertainty. In our words,

Gravity happens!

The danger from gravity is that you really have no control over when it will propel you or when it will pull you down a long fall to a final splat. Or do you? On September 17, 1989, gravity met Chris. He fell for 450 feet through the air before hitting the

Rescuing Bruce's gear from the crevasse on K2

2007 Shared Summits K2 Expedition, Don Bowie

side of the mountain. He bounced out and landed 50 feet later, like a dart stuck into a steep snow slope. He wasn't hurt.

Exactly ten years later, on September 17, 1999, gravity met Chris again. This time he was swept away by a giant avalanche on a peak in Tibet. Caught in the slide, he was twisted and crumpled and pushed to the very edge of the torrent. The wave of snow he was riding tossed him off to the side, burying him up to his neck. One hundred feet below Chris, the main flow of the avalanche roared over a cliff edge. Again, Chris wasn't hurt.

Chris was lucky—a lot. And hence we discover the survival tip for the final danger, called gravity: luck.

Survival Tip: Luck

Location: K2, continued

As soon as Bruce disappeared, the rope whipped tight. Two hundred pounds of climber and gear were pulling me by the waist. I fought with all my strength, but it was of no use. I was being dragged toward the bottomless crevasse he fell into.

Bruce's foot had pushed straight through a snow bridge, one he didn't even know was there. He was now falling straight down, through a hole no wider than his shoulders

He was expecting me to stop him.

I couldn't. I was holding the rope and trying to dig my feet into the surface of the snow, but I couldn't get any grip. I was on the losing team in a life-or-death tug-of-war. I knew I was going to be pulled into Bruce's crevasse, and then we would both tumble into the darkness, bouncing from side to side between the icy walls until we were wedged in place. If we survived the 200-foot fall, the cold would kill us.

I was still on the surface, being dragged along the path Bruce had just made, when suddenly the snow exploded around me.

I was hurtling into another hidden crevasse. Seconds before Bruce had walked right across this one, and the bridge held his weight. Now, miraculously, it opened up and swallowed me whole. The rope stopped my fall with a jerk. The impact forces slammed me into the crevasse wall. And then everything slowed down. Hanging on the rope, I slowly twisted in a small arc, banging my right hip into the wall. Looking up, I could see the edge of my hole, five feet above me.

The tightened rope went straight from my harness, through that hole, and across the flat glacier, before bending over the edge of Bruce's crevasse, to where he lay dangling some twenty-five feet below the surface. Both crevasses seemed bottomless.

We were alive. In the history of mountaineering, there probably isn't another story like this one: two men fall in two separate crevasses, saving their lives.

Admit it: luck plays a big role in all of our successes. Like every other aspect of life, success in extreme environments depends on three factors: luck, strategy, and execution. Sometimes you should be killed but aren't. You were simply lucky. Similarly, bad things happen to all of us, for no apparent reason. More miraculously, somehow we escape.

During the dot-com era or the real estate boom, few people called it right. But during those gold rushes, everyone seemed brilliant. And the high-tech CEOs, house flippers, and mortgage brokers were superstars. But isn't everyone a genius or a superstar when gravity is propelling us and our industry is on fire? At times like this, a buffoon makes money by just showing up for work. But when gravity starts to suck, so do we. At the point when it all collapses, we disappear into the abyss of hopelessness. What can a high altitude leader possibly do?

If you're working in a hot industry (say, the candy business in late October, or the turkey business in late November, or the toy industry in early December), gravity works with you. But many of us don't have the luxury of betting our career growth, project rollouts, or stock price on such predictability. Sometimes we win, and sometimes we lose. Then we rationalize why we're so brilliant, or why we're so stupid, or why we were victimized. But what we don't do enough of is accept the role that luck plays in our successes.

High altitude leaders accept luck as part of the success equation. You see, there are two kinds of games: games of chance and games of skill. Chutes and Ladders is a game of chance. You can practice every day, and there is still no way to improve your odds of winning. You just have to hope that you get a lucky spin of the dial. Monopoly is a game of skill. Yes, you still roll the dice, but the shrewd buying and selling of real estate is where the game is won or lost.

Since there are two kinds of games, there are two kinds of luck:

- *Skill-based luck:* The luck you create—as in the old saying, "Luck is what happens when opportunity and preparation collide," or Thomas Jefferson's version: "I'm a great believer in luck, and I find the harder I work, the more I have of it."
- *Pure luck:* The luck (good or bad) that just happens by chance.

Skill-Based Luck

The first type of luck is skill based. We've already discussed many of these skills: act in the face of real fear, subjugate your personal desires to the greater goal of the group, fight arrogance with humility, seek out and nurture partnerships, be seduced by passion and not by the tools, and persevere. When you combine these elements, you appear to be one lucky leader. Being viewed as lucky, you attract even more good fortune. As your good fortune grows, others will say you're on a lucky streak. But we know that all this luck comes from the application of hard-earned skills and a positive mental attitude.

We can't say enough about the need to have a positive mental attitude to increase skill-based luck. Cynics and curmudgeons do not inspire peak performance in their teams. Depressed teams do not see possibilities. Ask anyone who is negative, and they'll tell you they aren't lucky.

If you crash-land a plane in the Amazon or wash up on a desert island, what's the single most important tool you will need to survive? A positive mental attitude. The skills of survival aren't too complicated, but the willingness to survive, especially in the worst of circumstances, is critical. Many companies screen for attitude in their hiring process. You can teach skills, but it's hard to teach attitude. Certainly it can be done, but does a company really have the time to spend on resetting someone's attitude so he or she can have better skill-based luck?

If we can be "lucky" at games of skill, we'll attract more and more opportunities. The self-help community and psychologists are onto something when they advocate taking control of your luck with a positive mental attitude. Olympic coaches, military leaders, the best counselors and teachers, and great managers know that the power of attitude differentiates same-skilled people into winners and losers. A scientist, aptly named Professor Wiseman, set out to prove why some people are lucky and others are not. He conducted ten years of research and found the following four insights people use for becoming lucky:[3]

- *Maximize chance opportunities by being open to new experiences.* Increase your chances that something good will happen by creating, noticing, and acting on chance opportunities. Do this by "building and maintaining a strong network, adopting a relaxed attitude to life, and being open to new experiences." These can help you notice chance opportunities when they happen.

- *Listen to your lucky hunches: Your gut is normally right.* Feel and act on hunches about people or situations. Use your intuition. Take steps to boost your intuitive abilities, for example, "by meditating and clearing your mind of other thoughts."

- *Expect good fortune, and visualize yourself being lucky.* "Lucky people are certain that the future will be bright. Over time, that expectation becomes a self-fulfilling prophecy because it helps lucky people persist in the face of failure and positively shapes their interactions with other people." Before an important meeting or telephone call, expect good fortune.

- *Turn bad luck into good.* "Lucky people employ various psychological techniques to cope with, and even thrive upon, the ill fortune that comes their way." Lucky people imagine how things could have been worse and don't dwell on ill fortune. They take control of the situation. They may even spend a few moments each day remembering things that went well. Lucky people use "psychological techniques to cope with, and often even thrive on, the ill fortune that comes their way."

If you regularly experience skill-based "luck," you deserve to pat yourself on the back. It lets us know that you are tuned in to real possibilities, even if you can't put your finger on why you were lucky this time.

But is there a sixth sense for luck? We believe we are aware of certain truths on a subconscious level. Chris observed an example of Wiseman's trust-your-gut insight after his own lucky break in the fall of 1999 after being picked up and safely dumped by the wayside by that huge avalanche. A few weeks later, he went to a second Tibetan mountain, Shisha Pangma. The day he arrived at base camp, a large group of American climbers was already at the higher advanced base camp. After six days of constant snowfall, they were eager to scout the route to the base of the mountain. Six members of the team skirted the edge of the glacier, while the three most experienced climbed onto the glacier, taking a shortcut. Six thousand feet above them, a small avalanche started. As it tumbled down the mountain, it tripled in size, then tripled again and again. Now, a tsunami of snow and ice, 1,000 feet wide and a dozen feet thick, raced down the mountain. The three climbers on the glacier ran for their lives, while far below, their six friends watched in horror.

These three climbers were arguably the most experienced American mountaineers. Two of them ran straight down the slope. Perhaps they thought they could outrun the avalanche, or maybe they were headed for the shelter of a serac. The third ran across the slope toward the glacier's edge. He was picked up by the avalanche, sucked along, tumbled, and bruised, but he escaped with his life. The other two are buried in the ice.

Why would two men choose to run down the hill and one choose to run across the slope? In the very instant, they didn't have time to think. They just knew to run. One man's intuition about which direction to run saved him.

All of the climbers in base camp went to aid that team. They spent a stormy day hiking to advanced base camp and carrying the American team's gear back down. Chris spent a lot of those hours with a Russian mathematician. They discussed the odds of surviving in the Himalayas. At that time, the death-to-summit ratio on Shisha Pangma was 11 percent, making it one of the safer of the world's tallest peaks.

The surviving climber didn't have any time to think through his options; he just went in the direction that his subconscious told him to. Talk to seasoned leaders, and they'll tell you of times when their gut told them one thing even though the facts presented a different perspective. Sometimes they followed their gut, and sometimes they didn't. Their gut instinct was right more often than it was wrong. There's no magic formula to make the decision of choosing your gut over the presented facts, but ignore your gut at your peril.

Pure Luck

But what about the second kind of luck? When the forces of gravity switch directions, let's just hope that the dial we spin puts us on a good luck, not a bad luck, square. Remember in the opening story of this chapter that it was bad luck that Bruce fell into that first crevasse. If Bruce and Chris weren't crossing that glacier so soon after the snow fell, they would have seen tell-tale signs of the crevasse's existence. Chris wouldn't have been caught in that avalanche in 1999 if they had a weather forecast telling them of the impending storm. And Chris wouldn't have fallen for 450 feet off that peak in India if he had checked the ropes before he leaned back on them.

In all three of those instances, human error contributed to the event, but Chris had no control over the outcomes. Why did a second crevasse suddenly appear and swallow Chris up? Why did the avalanche push Chris out of harm's way just seconds before pouring over the cliff edge? How did Chris fall so far and manage to hit a patch of snow instead of one of the many rocks?

There's no explanation for luck.
Both good and bad luck occur as teams seek the summit.
You can lead your team and do it all correctly with no mistakes,
and still be swept over a cliff by an avalanche.

A friend once told us of the zero-sum theory of luck: if you're getting it, that means some else ain't. Of course, the context of that conversation was dating. As with dating, everyone gets a turn at being lucky. Some are just luckier than others. Let's just hope you're playing against the singer/songwriter David Bromberg, who said at a concert that Chris attended, "If it wasn't for bad luck, I'd have no luck at all."

Does this affect your career or company? You bet it does. In fact, Rosenzweig says it best: "Chance often plays a greater role than we think, or than successful managers usually like to admit."[4]

Good luck!

Key Learnings

- We are all hard at work in a world that is governed by gravity. Sometimes gravity propels us; at other times, it sucks us down.

- In games of skill (for example, business and relationships), there are ways that we can enhance our luck.

- In games of chance, we are at the whim of gravity.

Dan and Austin, after the storm, on the ledge at 19,000 feet on Mount Shivling

Chris Warner

Danger #9

THE JOURNEY BEGINS

Location: Mount Shivling, India

Death

The wind races across the mountain threatening to pull us from our ledges at 19,000 feet high. Though encrusted in a thickening layer of ice, the snow still filters into our sleeping bags. Our body heat melts the snowflakes, making the sleeping bags and clothes even wetter. Every hour that passes, the ice grows closer to our skin. Sooner or later, we will freeze and die.

My two friends shiver four feet above me on a table-sized rock, pressed against each other, cocooned in the fetal position. They are hit directly by every gust. To their left, the wall drops 5,000 feet to the next level. Below them on their right, I'm on a ledge no wider than a phone book and am hit only by the updrafts and eddies, my back against the granite wall. My feet are slotted behind a flake of rock. My hip rests on a ledge of ice, sculpted by centuries of Himalayan winds. To my right, the cliffs fall away for 2,000 feet, ending on small plateau just big enough to hold a steeply tilted glacier. The summit is 1,800 feet above us. And our empty base camp, which we left four days before, is miles away.

We're trapped by the storm and have nowhere to hide.

It sucks.

The storm hit us with little warning. In fifteen minutes, the sky darkened, the temperatures plummeted below zero, and the storm hit us head-on. We had reached a vertical granite wall, the crux of a route renowned for its difficulty. The day before, we had climbed for sixteen hours before giving up the hope that we'd find any ledge. Instead we dug three cryptlike trenches, four feet long, on the very crest of a knife-edged ridge. Our feet dangled over the edge. We thought that was a horrible camp, but at least we had enough space to lie side by side and use our tiny stove to melt snow into water.

When the storm hit, we knew we needed shelter, but we couldn't find any ledges big enough to hold a tent. So we left our ropes anchored in place and rappeled down to the cramped ledge system we had passed hours earlier.

That's how we got here, on a peak called Shivling.

Shivling is named for the penis of the Hindu god of destruction. It's a mountain rich not just in mountaineering lore, but in Hinduism's colorful past. It sits beside Mount Meru, the center of the universe. The melt waters of Shivling and Meru trickle downhill, forming the start of the Ganges River system.

Arrogance and Death

My two friends and I had known each other for years and had chosen this remote peak for a reason. It was rumored to be among the most challenging mountains in the world, a peak whose history reads like a who's who of Himalayan hard men. If we could climb Shivling, we could climb anything.

Now we knew why. Here we are: three young friends, thousands of feet up a notorious granite phallic symbol with a blizzard in full fury, fighting against the odds and gods for our very lives.

On the second day, the storm still rages on. Then, as if nothing could get worse, we drop our cook pot. It falls with a clatter, but is quickly silenced by the thickly falling snow. By noon I start to hallucinate from the exhaustion and hypothermia. The day passes slowly as we shovel handfuls of snow out of our sleeping bags, shivering to create warmth.

As darkness descends, we fall into fitful sleeps from which we might never awake. Death will surely start to take us, one by one.

On the third morning, we are still alive. The storm seems to change. Before, the clouds stayed high above us, dropping an endless supply of snow across the mountains. But now the clouds are wrapped all around us, so thick that daylight barely penetrates. The snow and the sounds, however, echo a change in the storm. The snow magically forms in the air around us, so close that gravity can't add the speed needed for the icy flakes to sting when they hit our skin. The winds have dropped, considerably; the sound of hurricane forces and the sandblasting of snow against nylon is replaced by the deep rolling thunder of avalanches below us.

Luck
By 8:00 A.M. shafts of sunlight slice through the clouds. We slowly venture just inches from our cocoons of frozen nylon and down. Sitting up for the first time in days, we begin to talk to each other. Is it possible we might live?

As the mountain is swept by dozens of avalanches below, we know it will take days to shed the two or three feet of fresh snow. If we try to descend by the route we spent three days climbing, we will certainly die. Our only hope is to go up the mountain, climb across thousands of feet of nearly vertical granite, and descend a long, twisting ridgeline on the other side of the mountain.

Adaptation
But we had dropped our cook pot. The only food we have left are nine Twix bars—not the double-wide bars but the individually wrapped single sticks that the Mars Corporation had donated. To melt water, we improvise and fashion a small pot with a piece of tinfoil. After not eating or drinking anything for more than forty hours, we feast on a single Twix bar and sip a half cup of tea.

Then we accept our only option for survival: going straight up.

Can you imagine being in a more desperate situation? Well, it got worse.

By 10:00 A.M., we shoulder our packs and head up. The clouds close in on us again, the snow falls, and the wind blows. We climb back up the icy ropes. I go first, hoping that the ropes haven't been damaged during the storm. Where the rock rises vertically, I spin on icy ropes, twisting slowly like a sail as the wind pushes against my pack. I look up and get a face full of snow. The thick clouds filter all the blue out of the light, turning the rocks, snow, and even our skin a tornado green. The sense of everything about to spin out of control is overwhelming.

Partnership and Perseverance

At the top of the last rope, I head out into a great unknown, hoping to scrape my way across a thousand feet of near-vertical rock, plastered with discontinuous sheets of wet snow, by jamming sodden mittens, the pick of an ice ax, or the vertical points of steel crampons into any icy crack or onto any tiny horizontal ledge that I can find. Like all other climbers, we work as a partnership. I'm the leader: a rope stretches from my harness to the harness of my partners. When I'm 20 feet up from them, 20 feet of slack line connects us. If I fall, I would fall twice the distance of the slack in the rope. At 20 feet, I would fall 40. And at 150 feet, I would fall to my death. I can't afford to fall.

After eight hours of clinging to the rock face, we still can't find a ledge big enough to sit on. Total darkness now descends. We turn on our flashlights. I keep leading. And leading. And leading.

At 2:00 A.M. I fall for the first time. An icicle as thick and tall as a telephone pole collapses when I'm midway up it. Luckily I land in a drift of snow. Minutes later, I again fall from the same place.

Humility and Partnership

I was beaten.

I hand over the leadership role.

My partners take over as I rest up. Progress ensues. Two hours later, I take over leading the front again. Above me is the safety of a horizontal summit ridge. But between me and that ridge is a problem: a frozen wave of snow. It arches nearly 20 feet out over the mountain's face, and we're trapped beneath it. The only way up is to tunnel through the snow. I start to dig a vertical shaft, climbing up into the snow, excavating above my head with my ice axes. I will never forget looking down that shaft. The climbing rope trails between my legs, my crampons stick into the wall of the tunnel, and my back presses against the opposite wall. The beam of my flashlight disappears somewhere down the 6,000-foot vertical cliff I am precariously trying to escape. The darkness below seems bottomless.

Clawing my way to safety, I pop my head through the snow, then climb out of the hole and stagger toward the ridge crest. The rocks and ice are blanketed by loose snow, so there is nothing to anchor the ropes to. I dig a deep hole, sit down, lay my pack across my legs, and brace myself. My partners climb one by one up the shaft, with my body serving as our only anchor. After eighteen straight hours of climbing, we all can finally sit down.

We now try to set up the tent, hoping to sleep for a few hours. But more bad news: in our delirious state, we drop our tent poles, and they slide off the side of the mountain. Instead of sleeping, we brew a half cup of tea and eat a single Twix bar. A reluctant bit of sunlight tries to penetrate the clouds, painting the mountains around us with an unreal blue light. I feel as if I'm sitting in a Maxfield Parrish painting or a Disney movie. The peaks are animated, not real. I've never experienced such beauty. It's a mixture of the rarefied air of 21,000 feet, the ending gasps of a monsoon-fed storm system, and sunlight filtering through thousands of miles of the earth's atmosphere, all combining with exhaustion, dehydration, hypothermia, and a well-earned sense that we are, unbelievably, alive.

Now we only need to find a way to get down.

Compelling Saga and Perseverance

Instead of running for safer altitudes, we find ourselves consumed by the summit. It seems so close. Too exhausted to even chew our candy bars, we still have this burning desire to delay our descent by ascending a few more hundred feet of steep snow slopes. The detour will take at least two hours. Two of us decide to go for it. The third man is smarter.

Futility hits. We are stopped a dozen feet below the summit by a gap in the knife-edged ridge that challenges us. But we left all of our gear, the ropes and pitons, at the base of the slope. It's impossible to span the distance without hours of dangerous effort.

Humility

The goal is just feet away. But sometimes even when you are really close, the danger is not worth the extra effort.

We turn back.

From our packs, we walk across a gently sloped plateau that ends abruptly. We rig the ropes and rappel for 300 feet, spinning slowly when our feet can't touch the overhanging wall. We want to follow a narrow ridgeline that twists into a cloud bank if we are to avoid the avalanche zone. It's critical that we follow this route to get down safely.

But we don't.

I don't know what went wrong. Was it the rising clouds, or the thirty hours of nonstop climbing, or our starvation, or exhaustion? We had survived by adapting to everything nature threw at us. But this was a fateful mistake. Our first one.

We continue onward following our new, and more dangerous, route. But mistakes love company. Two thousand feet lower, rappeling 150 feet from every makeshift anchor, the second mistake happens, and it almost kills me. The ropes are anchored to an ice-covered rock. My partners lower themselves first. At the end of the rope, they bury their ice axes into the deep snow and wait. I lean back, letting my weight ease onto the rope. I've rappeled a thousand times. It is always the same: a small taste of fear tickles your soul as you lean over the edge, but as soon as the rope pulls tight against your harness, a feeling of acceptance eclipses all anxieties.

This time that feeling lasts only for a moment.

Death

It takes five and a half seconds to fall 450 feet, a long time when you're falling. It becomes long enough to think: *I am not in control, and losing control means certain death. But death is not an option. Control must be reclaimed. I need a plan, a good plan! Remember what's below. How can I stop on that steep slope, before that field of crevasses? If I land there, they will never find my body. I'll rot or be eaten by vultures. So I have to stop. But I can't let my crampons hit because they will dig in and shatter my legs. I have to dig my hands in first, deep into the snow slope, like a go-cart brake, and slowly push them deeper because a sudden stop might tear my arms from their sockets. I have to stop, I have to live.*

Luck and Partnership

My body reaches 111 miles per hour when I finally slam into the snow slope. I don't even know what part of my body hit first. I bounce. Fifty more feet through the air, and I land again, like a dart. My legs thrust deep into the snow. My torso whiplashes back. But I'm buried too deep to fall again.

But then it gets worse. I now realize that my first fall triggered an avalanche. Flying through the air, I had outraced it. But now, buried past my knees, I am in its path and cannot move. I face death again. The avalanche sweeps over me. The weight of the snow pushes me farther back, and my spine twists with the impact. I feel the snow piling on my chest, heavier by the second.

Finally, it's over. The avalanche washes past me, and I'm facing uphill. I can suddenly see! And the sight is frightening. One of my partners is tumbling down the slope headed right at me. Had I hit him? Did I kill him on impact? At this point, it doesn't matter. His body is headed directly toward me. Even though I survived the first fall and the avalanche, in a second I will be falling again.

But then he twists. He's alive! He somehow gets his feet below him, his head uphill, and he claws at the slope, digging in with his hands. He stops sliding just a few feet above me. Tears in his eyes, fear shaking his body, he climbs down to me.

I'm a mess but alive, and the only reason I am alive is because of my partner. When he saw my body arc into the sky, he grabbed the ends of the rope. Seconds later, as the rope tightened with the brutal force of my falling body, he was pulled from the slope. The ropes tore from his hands. But in that split second that our bodies fought against each other, my trajectory was changed. Because he pulled, I fell only those 450 feet and reached a maximum speed of only 111 mph. If he hadn't grabbed the ends of the rope, I might have fallen for 600 or 700 feet. I might have hit a rock or ice instead of soft snow. He pulled; I bounced.

Humility

I suffer only one physical injury from that fall: a small scratch on my nose that barely bleeds. But I'm still damaged goods. All I want to do is sob. My heart is so heavy and my nerves so frayed that I want to cry like a baby. But I know that if I do, I will die. We had been on the move for nearly thirty-two hours. Before that, we had spent forty-six hours trapped on a tiny ledge. We had been battered by storms for seventy hours. And in the past seventy-six hours, we've eaten just two Twix bars and drunk eight ounces of water. My partners didn't have the strength to carry me. I have to get myself off this mountain. I can't cry. It will kill me.

We're all a wreck, but this is no time for self-pity. Darkness is only minutes away, and we're hours from a place safe enough to spend the night and over a day away from base camp.

Bravery

I don't know how, but I find the courage and suppress the tears. At first I can hold them back for a few seconds. Slowly those seconds stretch longer. Little did I know at the time, but it will take me weeks to work through that need.

We descend into the night, clawing our way across a near-vertical wall of ice and snow for hours. Finally we arrive back at that twisting ridge, the route we knew would get us safely down. We dig a ledge just big enough for the three of us. We fold a scrap of tinfoil into a pot. Snow is melted. We each drink a half cup of tea and fall asleep.

Hours later, a small chunk of ice falls from somewhere up above. It hits a pocket of snow, triggering a crack system that radiates with the speed of a gunshot, traveling through the snowpack and releasing an avalanche. More than a mile wide, the avalanche sweeps over the very cliff I fell from earlier, hits the slope that stopped me, and scours the snow we traversed across. In only seconds, the mountain is swept clean. The snow pushes with such force that individual flakes, thrown into the air, form a thunderhead of a cloud. For minutes we watch the cloud grow taller and wider. Then as the power drains from the air, the snowflakes fall, burying us in inches of icy dust.

Time to get moving. We pack our sleeping bags, rappel off one more cliff face, and stagger for seven hours, finally reaching base camp.

We spent seven days climbing Shivling and never touched the summit. But when I look back on my career as a mountaineer, a guide, and an entrepreneur, no other adventure better describes a process to overcome seemingly insurmountable challenges. It possesses all the elements: a compelling saga, great partners, a willingness to adapt to ever-changing realities, humility, courage, and overcoming our fears.

If you substituted your own story into mine, how would it read? Would you have recognized the dangers and taken the appropriate survival measures? More important, is it too soon to reflect on your own life and ask yourself:

**"When have I laid it all on the line to make
my dream come true?"**

If you never have, are you playing too safe? Are you pushing yourself to new levels? What challenges before you require more courage to overcome than you feel you possess? If this were a matter of life or death, would your actions allow you to survive?

Tom's Story: Survival in Career and Business

One of the better examples of survival in career and business is the life of Tom Gildee. Tom was a member of a CEO group that Don facilitated in Baltimore during the early 1990s. Tom was the founder and CEO of VIPS, an incredibly successful information systems company that he then sold to become a philanthropist.[1] Tom was abandoned by his mother when he was five years old. He never knew his father. Raised by his grandmother on welfare, Tom was fated for a long, hard life—if he lived that long at all. But then something happened. This is his story.

Luck

My grandmother got me enrolled in St. Ambrose parochial school. It was a pretty good break for me because I got a good education and discipline. But I was still a hellion. Some nuns believed in me; others thought I was just a lot of trouble. By the time I was in eighth grade, I was banned from graduation because I told them I didn't believe in God. But I was pretty smart because I was dead set on knowing stuff academically. Because of that, I was one of only two kids of sixty who got accepted at Baltimore Polytechnic Institute, one of the nation's top engineering high schools. It was an honor. I got a really good education for about two and a half years, and that's when the wheels came off the cart.

Gravity

My grandmother died. I started drinking and got arrested five times. My sense of inferiority from not having a father or mother got to me. I felt something was wrong with me, and I got much-craved attention by getting in trouble. The world sucked. I ended up living in five homes in eighteen months. After being passed around to various family members, I was at the end of the line. I ended up at my friend Joe's house.

Luck

Joe's mom was a big part of saving my life. She was a lovable Italian, and she had this line you didn't cross. I finally had some structure. It got me through to the twelfth grade, and I graduated from high school. But graduating was in itself a mess. I ended up being a screwup in school. So they kicked me out of the A-course and gave me a B-course diploma; the B-course was the lower level of achievement. I didn't care. I just wanted to get out of high school. I was totally rudderless. I needed money, so I got a job at an insurance company that I got just with an aptitude test, and I started programming computers. Then I got drafted.

Luck Again

Getting drafted saved my life.

But as usual, I kept screwing up. Not many people go into the service as a private and come out as a private. I had about forty days left before I got out when I drank a fifth of bourbon on guard duty. Apparently the military thinks guard duty is important. I apparently didn't. An officer checked up on me, and I was so drunk I put my rifle on lock and load; it was loaded and ready to fire. I marched him to the fence, and as a young kid, I'm sure he thought he was going to die. He tricked me and got away. Then I was surrounded by five military police trucks and proceeded to have the crap kicked out of me. I was put in jail.

They were going to court-martial me, and two years in the stockade would've killed me. But my company commander was a black officer, which was unusual because it was rare to see a black officer back in those days. He saw something in me, a young black man, and wanted to save me. It was a miracle. I was on the edge of my life. He went and argued for me and got me off. He saved my butt.

What really got me on line in life is that they busted me down to no stripes and put me on guard duty for thirty days, with two hours on and four hours off. It was like torture. But in my sleep-deprived daze, I had a lot of time to think about myself. And then I got it! Like a heroin addict who crashes for a third time, I knew that if I didn't get my act together, I was going to die. That's what changed my life: that last break from that officer.

All that negative energy I had got totally transformed. I left the military, got a job as a trainee programmer, and graduated from Johns Hopkins University. That was all I needed. I was on fire. I learned everything I could. I loved it. They didn't even have to pay me. I couldn't believe how much fun working and helping people was. I ended up working for the government programming systems, handling Medicare claims processing.

Compelling Saga

What made it fun? Creating these wonderful software systems to make people's life easier. It was a terrific turn-on—not just coming up with a solution, but coming up with a grand, elegant solution. That's what I loved doing, and have since for my whole career. I didn't just want to solve a problem but wanted to solve it in a different, more elegant way.

Eventually Ross Perot's EDS company came into the business of facilities management and first targeted Medicare systems. Now I was not only creating software but also had a cause: to kick Ross Perot's butt! Our system captured twenty-five states before Ross went to Congress to make the case that the government shouldn't be creating software. Obviously he had an agenda.

In 1975 the edict came down that we were out of business, but shutting down a government program takes a lot of time. In 1976 I said to my boss that I didn't have a lot to do, but one of our clients needed a new field on their screen and I'd like to add it. But more so, I'd like to re-create the entire system. I wanted to do something great. He said, "Gildee, look, I've long given up trying to control you. Whatever you do, just don't make a big deal about it." I created a great system, but eventually I had to go too. And I was going to get another job when one of our clients said, "Are you crazy? You've got this software out here and no one to maintain it. You need to create a company."

Partnership

I called up George, whom I had worked with at a bank earlier, and off we went. I had worked with George before, and he was a tough hombre. He's a guy who would never say die. I knew I needed someone I could rely on. I am very creative, but I needed someone else, and that was George. That how VIPS (Viable Information Processing Systems) got started.

VIPS is the little engine that could. I'm proud that it's been bought and sold several times by many companies, including WebMD. But the entire company is self-contained and was never disemboweled. Very unusual for a company to do that. It's a great company.

Perseverance

Looking back, probably what I've described to you is that perseverance in overachieving was my strategy for survival. Everyone has a survival strategy to be loved and accepted. That was mine.

In a sense, Tom's personal saga to create great, elegant solutions gave him what he needed to persevere through the toughest of obstacles. And with a lot of luck, he was successful. He eventually ended up with $15 million and, true to form, put his wealth into Kids Are VIPS. He now gives kids who are at risk major breaks by doing things like getting them into good schools. He's given hundreds of breaks, passing on the luck that he got in his life. "If I can give one kid a break," he says, "it's worth it." Luck goes around.

Now that you know the dangers and how to survive them, there's no excuse not to become the leader you could be. But before you continue the climb, we have a few insights to share. In our struggles to build our businesses or develop our careers, we easily forget that we are, after all, human. You will sometimes set the bar too high, and the expectations a team places on you as a high altitude leader can be even higher. They expect that you will wield your power with honor, integrity, and humility. As you strive and stumble and risk the journey ahead, the following final thoughts will help.

Beware the Three Small Mistakes

"How did you go bankrupt?"
"Gradually, then suddenly."
—*Ernest Hemingway*, The Sun Also Rises

In mountaineering, rarely does the first error kill a climber. Death occurs when the third thing goes wrong. For example, running out of oxygen is survivable, but not if a storm catches you up high and poor visibility causes you to become lost. At some point, you will sit down, fall asleep, and, at forty degrees below zero, freeze solid in six hours.

On big peaks, we tell clients that the first mistake they made was joining the expedition. They are now in an environment where things can go terribly wrong very quickly. If they are going to make it home alive, they have to be more disciplined, more giving, and more humbled than ever before. Everybody has to scan the horizon. Everyone has to examine themselves and each other for signs of weakness. Everyone is responsible for their own safety and the safety of everyone else. They have to prevent the small mistakes from adding up to a catastrophe.

Just as in mountaineering, business leaders make small errors almost daily. But how many does it take before the errors reach a deadly magnitude of bringing down a project, or a career, or a company? Both organizations and expeditions fail because a series of mistakes build on themselves, and before anyone notices. How many teams failed before anyone realized that the demoralized culture, increased customer dissatisfaction, and hemorrhaging profits would combine into an inescapable landslide? No single snowflake thinks it's responsible for the avalanche.

Dangerous, unproductive, dysfunctional (DUD) behaviors resemble these kinds of mistakes and often cause an organization's slow death. Beware of them throughout your journey to high altitude.

> DUD behaviors in organizations don't
> hit you like an avalanche.
> They creep up on you.

What's the situation like in your company? Take a walk around and notice how many DUD patterns are creeping up right now:

- Sure, Chuck violated one of the company's published values. But he's a nice guy. No one will notice if you do nothing.

- Stacey should be fired. You've lost confidence and trust in her capabilities. But it's too uncomfortable to deal with right now. You're busy, and no one else realizes the problem. It's okay to wait.

- Jack's selling to the wrong customers; he's not supporting the new strategy. But he's been here forever and knows he can do it his way. He's got seniority. If you let him go, it'll cause too much of a backlash in the company. Best to just tolerate his behavior.

- Someone should tell the boss that her policy is costing the company money and time. Maybe someone else will give her the bad news.

- How close are you, your team, or your company to reaching the three small mistakes that will eventually become a deadly combination for your career or your profits?

Keep the Passion Alive

If you do anything next after reading this book, create your own personal compelling saga that inspires you to become a high altitude leader. You can't infect others with passion unless you're infected yourself. What story or drama captures your epic journey? What significant goal is left for you to do in life?

Driven by a compelling saga, you'll endure extreme hardships and won't get distracted from becoming a high altitude leader by a conflicting desire for some fleeting pleasure. Once you taste the deeper satisfaction that comes with this kind of effort, you'll become an addict, seeking high performance from every part of life. You'll be a pusher too, dragging along every disciple who has the guts to play with you. Employees who get caught up in this enthusiasm love to work with passionate people because their work, no matter how mundane, becomes important. We know this is true from the studies of athletes. When athletes face the greatest opponents and their very best is demanded, they block out external distractions and enter into a hyperperformance zone that psychologists call the flow state. Freed from self-doubt and the other burdens of the ego, they experience the deepest level of satisfaction even as they are engaged in the fiercest of battles. Once athletes experience the flow state (also called the championship zone) they spend their careers training themselves to return to it.

Tom Gildee remembers his flow state: "When I look back, once I could see the design, I got it and knew where I wanted to get to. My body didn't care what I had to go through. One hundred hours per week, no problem. I was 100 percent focused. I remember those states clearly. It's almost like if you're not 100 percent focused now and totally consumed by it, you can't create it."

As a leader, you probably already know what the flow state is like. We've all experienced it. Remember those times when you felt at one with the task? You didn't have to think; you just acted, and everything seemed to fall into place. Afterward you felt deep satisfaction, knowing that you were at the top of your game. There was no need to gloat or brag. It would have ruined the moment.

Imagine what work would be like if you could return to that level of performance every day. Imagine how great it would be if your team regularly performed like that. That would be a high-performance team, the holy grail of leadership.

And as you rise higher, don't forget to care for those around you. Take care of each other.

Location: K2, continued

On K2, when we found the dying Czech climber and carried him for a thousand feet to our tent, it was clear to us that we needed to cram four big guys into a tent made for three. It was just one of many sacrifices we made, giving it little thought. Don crawled in first to start treating him, while Bruce went from tent to tent finding some critically needed hot water. I gave up my sleeping bag (even though the temperature dipped well below zero) and stayed awake for an additional two hours, melting snow so everyone would have water.

The next day, the strongest climbers (the Portuguese, the Russian, and the Koreans) left Camp 4 as soon as they were ready. At least one of these teams left knowing that the Italian climber was lost in the storm and that the exhausted Czech lay in our tent. They left Don, Bruce, and me to care for the Czech, the Italians, and the Iranian. The strongest climbers were in base camp by dinner.

And the rest of us caring for the injured?

It was three days before we finally made it back.

In the most extreme situations, true leadership emerges in the self-sacrifice that people exhibit for others. We call it altruism. If we can be altruistic, can't we expect the same of our teammates?

Samuel Oliner is a Holocaust survivor who knows a lot about altruism in extreme situations, and how selfish agendas can be overridden. A professor at Humboldt State University and founder of the Altruistic Personality and Prosocial Behavior Institute, Oliner says:

Altruism simply means devotion to the welfare of others, based on selflessness. Specifically, I have characterized altruism as a behavior that is directed towards helping another; that involves some effort, energy, and sacrifice to the actor; that is accompanied by no external reward; and that is voluntary. I divide altruism into two categories: conventional and heroic. Conventional altruism differs from heroic only in that it does not usually entail risk to the life of the helper.[2]

The compelling sagas driving such altruistic behavior probably had their inception in the values and principles instilled by the parents of such people. Similarly, organizational values can drive the same outcomes and behavioral traits. Oliner's team has identified the key traits found in conventional altruism, which we believe best mirror the realm we see in organizations (luckily, most employees don't risk their lives at work):

- Courage
- Moral code
- Efficacy
- Social responsibility
- Honor
- Patriotism
- Virtue
- Valor
- Normative group affiliation

Leaders are presented with a million opportunities to practice altruism every day. Liberty Mutual has a popular television commercial campaign airing as we write this. It shows "ordinary" people going a step or two out of their way to help someone else. One person's small act makes an impression on another person, who then steps forward. It is a great commercial campaign. A fundamental difference between heroes and bystanders, Oliner says, is that heroes see the opportunity for action where bystanders see a hopelessly lost situation. They commit to succeed and accomplish the mission. They see a choice and cannot walk away.

You don't have to stumble on a dying Czech to practice altruism. You just have to control your selfish urge long enough to act for the good of the group. Acting once makes it easier to act again and again. Like exercise, you get stronger and stronger the more training you get. Wouldn't it be wonderful if folks started to use words like *courage, honor*, or *virtue* when describing you?

Proof of the possibility for inducing altruism resides in the graduate student programs we conduct at Earth Treks. We've been guiding leadership development expeditions for the Wharton School of Business for years. We take the M.B.A. candidates to climb big peaks in the Andes and Africa, where they are challenged to create a high-performance team. It's hard work, especially if you can't select your teammates. But time and again, the teams pull this off.

The key to success for the Wharton groups is framing the adventure as an altruistic compelling saga: get 100 percent of the team to the top, and safely back down. The extreme physical challenge this poses is demanding. Of the more than thirty of these expeditions we've run, only one team in the Andes and three teams on Kilimanjaro have reached the goal. But every group has learned more about leadership on those expeditions than they ever dreamed possible. Why do they fail but learn so much? For many:

- It's the first time they experience being part of a high-performance team—a revelation to most Type A people.
- Every person subjugates his or her personal desires to the higher goal of the group. Suddenly all the petty dramas stop, and the best in everyone comes out.
- They willingly alter their behavior because they know that they might die if anyone in their team screws up.

Not every team reaches its performance potential and not everyone gets it by the time the expedition is over. But for those who do, one thing is clear: individuals had to subjugate their personal desires if the group was to succeed. CEOs love hiring employees who can practice these values back in their company.

Don't Conquer the Peak; Conquer Yourself

On a Himalayan expedition with the writer Sam Keen, Don was struck by a comment he heard Keen make:

"It would be a shame to be born a man but die a CEO."

The statement raises a significant question for you. *Will you lose your true self in your quest to become great?* We hope not.

A Wharton Leadership Ventures Team on the summit of Mount Cotopaxi (19,348 feet)

Chris Warner

Lose yourself, and you have nothing left. If this book has at least raised this question in your mind, it has done its job. Remember that high altitude leaders don't seek to conquer the great goals; these are the results of their conquering themselves.

**Don't lose yourself in the process,
but dig deeper into yourself so that you can climb
ever higher.
This remains the timeless challenge of a leader.**

Each day you must engage the dangers inherent in the trek to higher altitudes. Surviving these dangers ensures your personal success and the breathless views from the summits you reach. As a leader, you owe it to yourself, your team, and your company to be ever vigilant so that all may summit—and then make it safely back to base camp.

Well, we knocked the bastard off!
—*Edmund Hillary, on first climbing*
Mount Everest

Resources

The world is ever changing. Please make sure you visit us often at www.HighAltitudeLeadership.com for:

- A free personal high altitude leadership assessment
- Free support tools for your career and team
- Information on joining a mountaineering expedition
- The latest information on Don and Chris's research
- Additional chapter content (if you enjoyed this book, you'll love what we have for you on our Web site)

If you want to bring this work into your industry or company, visit www.HighAltitudeLeadership.com for programs to accelerate performance, including:

- Keynote speeches for companies and industry conferences
- Advanced outdoor leadership training events
- Compelling saga creation
- Rescue operations for failed change programs
- Superior executive team development
- Culture and accountability alignment
- Employee training and development
- Strategic planning

Notes

Chapter One

1. Quoted in K. Weekes, *Women Know Everything! 3,241 Quips, Quotes, and Brilliant Remarks* (Philadelphia: Quirk Books, 2007), p. 155.
2. L. Gonzales, *Deep Survival: Who Lives, Who Dies, and Why* (New York: Norton, 2003).
3. B. Burrough and J. Helyar, *Barbarians at the Gate: The Fall of RJR Nabisco* (New York: HarperCollins, 1990).
4. From D. Schmincke, *The Code of the Executive* (New York: Plume, 2000), p. 1. "Death may seem an unlikely topic today. Upon reflection, we arrive at a different conclusion. First, medical research shows how stressed lifestyles from conflicting priorities, time constraints, stressful decisions, career threats, poor nutrition, lack of exercise, and smoking, drinking, and other forms of drug addiction cause the early physical death of executives in the field of battle. Second, the organization itself can die at any time from competitive losses. Finally, the more serious death—the death of pride, arrogance, and self-importance—is as frightening as physical death. It is evident in the destructive power and political behavior that executives exhibit as they sacrifice good business decisions to preserve themselves. This is the death most feared, and the main killer of organizations. So, an executive warrior still needs to keep death firmly in mind.

For leadership he will die in pride and self-importance. For growth he will die in arrogance. For life he will die in the flesh."

Chapter Two

1. For more scientific data on this, see R. Dawkins, *The Selfish Gene* (New York: Oxford University Press, 1989).
2. V. Frankel, *Man's Search for Meaning* (New York: Simon & Schuster, 1984).
3. Compiled from personal experience, anecdotal research, and published work, including J. Collins and J. Porras, "Building Your Company's Vision," *Harvard Business Review*, Sept.-Oct. 1996, and G. Hamel and C. K. Prahalad, "Strategic Intent," *Harvard Business Review*, May-June 1989.

Chapter Three

1. From the international meeting of the Conference Board attended in the mid-1980s in New York City at the time when we were just starting out on our research. Eventually the data were published: M. Beer, "Why Change Programs Don't Produce Change," *Harvard Business Review*, Nov. 1, 1990.
2. http://www.armystudyguide.com/content/army_board_ study_guide_topics/leadership/troop-leading-procedures-nco .shtml.
3. For information on these instruments, go to www.HighAlt- itudeLeadership.com.
4. Competitive intelligence guru Benjamin Gilad, president of the Fuld Gilad Herring Academy of Competitive Intelligence, quoted in Air Tran's in-flight magazine: N. Learner, "I Spy: Keep Your Business on Track by Scouting Out the Competition—Legally," GO, Aug. 2007, p. 105.
5. See S. Holtz, and J. C. Havens, *Tactical Transparency: How Leaders Can Leverage Social Media to Maximize Value and Build Their Brand* (San Francisco: Jossey-Bass, forthcoming).

Chapter Four

1. The following quotations come from http://www.etni.org.il/quotes/predictions.htm.
2. http://www.adventurestats.com/tables/EverestO2Fat.shtml.
3. J. Krakauer, *Into Thin Air* (New York: Villard Books, 1997).
4. C. Fishman, "No Satisfaction at Toyota," *Fast Company*, Dec. 2006-Jan. 2007, no. 111, p. 84.

Chapter Five

1. The quotation was retrieved from http://www.mounteverest.net/news.php?id=10064.
2. From J. Biewen, "The Movie in Our Heads," *Revisiting Vietnam* (American RadioWorks, Apr. 2000), available at http://americanradioworks.publicradio.org/features/vietnam/us/movie.html. Also see Opinion Journal Archives, *Wall Street Journal*, at http://www.opinionjournal.com/best/?id=110010750: "In 1971 alone, there were 1.8 fraggings for every 1,000 American soldiers serving in Vietnam, not including gun and knife assaults."

Chapter Six

1. Quoted in S. Jayson, "Yep, Life'll Burst That Self-Esteem Bubble," *USA Today.com*, Feb. 15, 2005, http://www.usatoday.com/life/lifestyle/2005–02–15-self-esteem_x.htm.
2. From *Mercer Human Resource Consulting 2002 & 2005 What's Working Surveys*, as reported in MarketingHire.com: http://www.marketinghire.com/careers/surveys/1105/employee_commitment_rising.htm.

Chapter Seven

1. The Robert Heinlein quotation is available on most quotation Web sites. This one was retrieved from http://www.quotes-museum.com/quote/40145.

2. The Little quotation was retrieved from http://www.quotegeek.com/index.php?action=viewtheme&themeid=82.

Chapter Eight

1. E. Janszen, "The Next Bubble: Priming the Markets for Tomorrow's Big Crash," *Harpers*, Feb. 2008, p. 3.
2. P. Rosenzweig, *The Halo Effect . . . and the Eight Other Business Delusions That Deceive Managers* (New York: Free Press, 2007). Rosenzweig is a professor at the International Institute for Management Development (IMD) in Lausanne, Switzerland. He began his studies at the Wharton School of the University of Pennsylvania, receiving his Ph.D. in 1990. From 1990 to 1996, he was on the faculty of Harvard Business School, teaching business policy in the M.B.A. program. In 1996, he joined the IMD faculty.
3. The quotes that follow are from R. Wiseman, "The Loser's Guide to Getting Lucky," *BBC News*, http://news.bbc.co.uk/1/hi/magazine/3335275.stm; D. H. Pink, "How to Make Your Own Luck," *Fast Company*, no. 72, June 2003; and http://www.richardwiseman.com/research/moreluck.html/.
4. Rosenzweig, *The Halo Effect*, p. 174.

Chapter Nine

1. As of this writing, General Dynamics has agreed to buy VIPS for $225 million cash from its current owner, HLTH Corporation. PRNewswire-FirstCall, June 3, 2008.
2. S. P. Oliner, "Ordinary Heroes," *Yes Magazine*, Winter 2002.